# Classic Christmas

## True Stories of Holiday Cheer and Goodwill

Edited by
Helen Szymanski

Adams Media
Avon, Massachusetts

Published by Adams Media, an F+W Publications Company
57 Littlefield Street
Avon, MA 02322
*www.adamsmedia.com*

ISBN 10: 1-59337-520-4
ISBN 13: 978-1-59337-520-1

Printed in the United States of America.

J I H G F E D C B

**Library of Congress Cataloging-in-Publication Data**
Classic Christmas / edited by Helen Szymanski.
p.      cm.
ISBN 1-59337-520-4
1.  Christmas.  I. Szymanski, Helen.

GT4985.C5452 2006
394.2663--dc22

2006014716

This publication is designed to provide accurate and authoritative information with regard to the subject matter covered. It is sold with the
understanding that the publisher is not engaged in rendering legal,
accounting, or other professional advice. If legal advice or other expert
assistance is required, the services of a competent professional person
should be sought.
—From a *Declaration of Principles* jointly adopted by a Committee of the
American Bar Association and a Committee of Publishers and Associations

Many of the designations used by manufacturers and sellers to distin-
guish their products are claimed as trademarks. Where those designations appear in this book and Adams Media was aware of a trademark
claim, the designations have been printed with initial capital letters.

This book is available at quantity discounts for bulk purchases.
For information, please call 1-800-289-0963.

This book is dedicated to the Christ child for it is He who taught us love, and He whom we should honor each Christmas.

# Acknowledgments

A deeply felt thank-you is offered to all who have played a part in getting this book off the ground and into the hands of our readers. This thank-you extends to everyone at Adams Media, as well as to all my authors and all our readers, my family and friends, and everyone else who believed in me and in this book—you know who you are. And, finally, I'd like to thank God, who makes all things possible, for giving us the opportunity to bring these stories into your home.

A very special thank-you also goes to the following individuals who helped prepare the town spotlights, which appear in this book:

- Dianne Matthews and Susan Todd (Ripley, Tennessee)
- Joyce Anne Munn (Sciotoville, Ohio)
- Joan Rawlins Biggar Husby and Bill Rawlins (Robe, Washington)
- Janet Anderson Hurren (Perry, Utah)
- Janet Hounsell and Carla McAllister (Conway, New Hampshire)
- Lesa Cameron (Greenwood, Nebraska)
- J. Hogan Clark (Sedalia, Missouri)
- Norma Favor and John Paul Jamison (Beetown, Wisconsin)
- Ray Wong, Marsha Lloyd, and Pat Jones (Ridgecrest, California)
- Georgia Aker, Venita Shaw, Marty Magee, Jo Bond, Jerry Shaw, Gina Evans, and Monty Oney (Rayo, New Mexico)

# Contents

# Introduction

Christmas is my favorite time of the year. The holiday season is the perfect opportunity for my family to get together and share our love for one another, and that's where the real joy in the holiday lies—in the love we choose to share.

During my childhood years, I received many different types of gifts, but the presents that stand out in my mind are the ones that were simple and inexpensive. Perhaps I remember these particular gifts more fondly because they always came loaded with an extra heaping of love. I recall one year when several of my sisters and I each received a pair of red and white flannel pajamas covered with elves and toadstools. I'm guessing that the pajamas weren't top of the line, but they were warm and fuzzy, and they were covered with the very same elusive elves we daydreamed about and pretended to chase through the violets and across the meadow every day. Mom could not have found a better gift.

But that was Mom. She always seemed to know which gifts would be appreciated the most. I received my all-time favorite Christmas gift from her the year after I had gotten married. The gift was an old Mason jar with a metal lid and handle, filled with popcorn kernels. When I was a teenager, I popped popcorn for the whole family nearly every night. Additionally, since leaving home, I had begun collecting glass bottles, including old Mason jars. It meant the world to me that Mom remembered my favorite snack and also knew what my current likes were.

Though Mom was promoted to heaven nine years ago, I believe that her teachings live on in me and in each of her other fifteen children. When I need a reminder of what Christmas is all about, I look at the open shelf in my kitchen and see the very same Mason jar Mom gifted me with thirty years ago. The jar has long been empty of popcorn kernels, but it will always be filled with the knowledge that Christmas is not about how many expensive gifts you receive. I learned a very long time ago that Christmas is, always has been, and always will be about love.

—Helen Szymanski

# Sam

by J. Hogan Clark

Sedalia, Missouri

**W**hen he came to the door that day, I opened it and was a bit shocked at his appearance. Before me was an unkempt man, wearing dirty, ill-fitting clothes. On his head was a worn and soiled baseball cap with only a half decipherable insignia at the crown. He said his name was Sam, and he asked for my father by name, which I thought odd. I called my father to the door, left the two men to their discussion, and went about the business of a nine-year-old.

My father hired Sam to shovel the snow off our walkway that day. It was early December, and the winter of 1949 was unusually cold for our small Missouri town, with multiple snowstorms being strung together like beads in a necklace.

The homeless man appeared at our door on three more occasions that December, always asking for my father by name. Each time my father hired him to shovel our walkway. At his last appearance, I asked my father, a professional sign painter, about Sam.

My dad said he had met Sam the previous summer when he was painting a large sign on the side of a building. Sam had simply approached my father and begun talking. The mentally challenged man was pleasant enough and asked for nothing. He just wanted someone to talk to, and my father had obliged. After that, such meetings and conversation happened often between Dad and Sam.

In 1977, my father passed away. I had just returned to my mother's home for the funeral when there was a knock on the front door. I opened the door to a rather well-dressed white-haired lady. After introducing herself as an aide at the Veterans Administration Home in Kansas City, some distance from my hometown, she handed me a small gift-wrapped box. She expressed her condolences at my father's passing, and then she left.

I took the small package to my mother, seated in her living room, surrounded by friends and family, and informed her how it had come into my possession. My mother opened the package and found a World War II medal—a Purple Heart. There was a neatly folded, typed letter underneath the medal.

The letter had been typed by an aide of the Kansas City Veterans Home but was authored by a resident. The letter explained that the Purple Heart was the most prized possession of that resident and that he wanted my father to have it because my dad had been the only one who had talked to him. This, in turn, allowed him to earn enough money one cold winter to buy a pair of gloves for his mother's Christmas present.

At the bottom of the letter, in a barely legible scrawl, was the signature: Sam.

As a postscript, the aide had written that Sam had passed away and that the only thing he had owned was his Purple Heart—awarded to him during World War II military actions in Germany. Sam's last request had been to give the medal to my dad.

Sam's Purple Heart was placed in my father's coffin.

I learned much from my father, including the value of helping someone realize self-worth. I've never forgotten that lesson . . . and neither had Sam.

# Spotlight on Sedalia, Missouri

## Town Facts

**Population:** 20,269
**Location:** Sedalia is located 100 miles east of
Kansas City, 300 miles west of St. Louis,
and 18 miles south of Interstate 70, at the
junctions of U.S. 65 and U.S. 50.

## The History of Sedalia

Sedalia is steeped in history. Reminders of everything from the Civil War to the long-gone days when cowboys and cattle drives were the norm can be found in and around Sedalia.

In 1866, shortly after the Civil War, two railroads—the Missouri, Kansas, and Texas Line ("Katy") and the Missouri Pacific Line—helped guarantee a positive and lasting economic base for Sedalia.

Around the same time, Sedalia was also the destination of one of the great Texas cattle drives. Some 260,000 head of longhorn steers left Texas, making the journey up the Santa Fe Trail to the new railhead in Sedalia and Kansas City. The herd crossed Flat Creek, just south of Sedalia. Today, a bridge, erected in 1881, marks the spot.

## Jesse James and His Gang and the Great Train Robbery of 1876

Just a few miles east of Sedalia, near Otterville, is the site where the Missouri-Pacific train robbery took place on July 7, 1876. High on a bluff overlooking the Lamine River, Jesse James and his gang waited for their opportunity. As soon as the train slowed down to make the uphill grade, they jumped atop and quickly took control, robbing the train and its passengers of $17,000. A plaque is erected at the site, just off State Road AA, about three miles east of Otterville.

From the same bluff, the trenches along the Lamine River that were created during the Civil War are quite evident. The trenches, part of the "Wilderness Campaign" of the Civil War, were created by Union forces for protection from the Confederate soldiers, who were hoping to gain control of the railroads that converged in Sedalia.

## The Silver Screen Comes to Sedalia

Several of Sedalia's residents became celebrities, including Jack Oakie, a comedic film star of the 1930s. Oakie lived on 5th Street in Sedalia, prior to making his way to Hollywood and immortality. Sedalia was also home to Scott Joplin, a famous ragtime music composer. Joplin lived in Sedalia for many years and worked at the Maple Leaf Club on Main Street. It was there that he composed the famous *Maple Leaf Rag,* which was featured in the movie *The Sting.* Every year in June, Sedalia residents, along with other fans, celebrate Joplin's achievements at the annual Scott Joplin Festival.

Additionally, Clint Eastwood made the cowboy scene in Sedalia in the 1950s as "Rowdy Yates" from the television show *Rawhide* when he and his costar, Eric Fleming, visited Sedalia to kick off the series.

## Sedalia Today

Sedalia is the "State Fair City" for the annual Missouri State Fair, which has, since its inception, offered displays and held events that centered around Missouri agriculture and livestock industries. Held annually in August, the fair also features world-famous entertainers.

The Bothwell Mansion, north of Sedalia, still stands and is used by the State of Missouri as a museum with daily tours—May through September. The structure, originally built in the late 1800s by John H. Bothwell, a Sedalia lawyer and benefactor, is magnificent and a "must see" for visitors.

The railroad is still an important part of Sedalia. Originally a functioning passenger depot for the Missouri, Kansas, and Texas Railroads, the Katy Train Depot now houses a railroad museum and is a focal point for a statewide biking trail called "The Katy Trail." This trail is traversed by avid bicycle enthusiasts from all over the country. The site, restored to its original state, is beautiful and also houses the headquarters for Sedalia's Chamber of Commerce offices.

Sedalia has maintained its nostalgic past, to be sure, but it hasn't allowed itself to stagnate. Progress continues to surge forward, as can be seen in the many nationally known manufacturers, hotels, restaurant chains, retail establishments, and local businesses that have cropped up within Sedalia's borders.

These days Sedalia, Missouri, is a large enough town to provide all the amenities of comfort and convenience, yet small enough to assure the intimate camaraderie of neighbors and acquaintances.

## by Mary Helen Straker

Toys decorated the Christmas tree in the corner of the hospital classroom; the tree so real-looking you could almost smell pine needles. Tomorrow would be Christmas Eve, and it was beginning to look as though Tracy would be spending the holiday at home with Mark. She'd been back on her feet for nine days—after eight weeks of bed rest—and nothing had happened yet, much to the surprise of her doctor.

Tracy forced her thoughts away from the baby and onto the Lamaze teacher's words: *visualization, concentrate on imagery, free the mind from centering on the body.* Since she'd missed most of the classes, Tracy wanted to absorb all she could. She intended to deliver this baby perfectly.

"What does childbirth mean to you?" the RN asked. "Try to answer what most comes to your mind as we go around the class."

A girl, not more than sixteen, looked at her clenched fists—fingers bare of rings—and then at the floor. "Pain," she said softly, hunching her shoulders.

*Pain: The sound of babies crying as the nurses wheeled them in to their mothers. The physical pain of last year's miscarriage had scarred over, but other reminders were still raw.*

"Nurses!" said the curly haired man wearing a neck chain. Everyone laughed but Tracy.

*Nurses: The nurse telling Mark that evening, "You'll have to scrub and put on a gown. Your baby's in the room." He had stood in the doorway in the twilight until at last she'd whispered, "Mark . . . ," and he came across the room slowly to sit beside her and lay his cheek against hers in silence. The next morning, the nurse with the tiny parcel: "Here's your beautiful baby . . . oops! Sorry. Wrong room."*

"Diapers and wipers," said a man with a gray-streaked beard.

*Wipers: The cleaning woman, wastebasket in hand, "Have they brought your baby?" Tracy, turning her face away, could only shake her head. The wastebasket slammed, spilling, as the truth sank in.*

"Doctor." This time it was an older woman who spoke.

*Doctor: Tracy's doctor, consoling her. "Sometimes it's for the best. You're young. You must try again. Chances are good."*

"Life!" said a pretty brunette.

*Life: Being pregnant again. At fourteen weeks, the doctor asking, "Feeling life yet?" A small nudge that same evening, small, yet enough to move mountains. Mountains of hope. Then, into the third trimester, the pains came, which sent her to bed.*

"A goal," said the man with the what-am-I-doing-here look, tugging his mustache.

*A goal: She had marked off the days, the weeks, and the months—December—the goal at last within reach.*

"Beauty," said the redhead.

*Beauty: Mark had said yesterday, "When you coming out, Rascal? I want to see your beautiful face, sweet baby!"*

"A son!" said the lanky man. His wife shrugged, widening her eyes. Had she, like Tracy and Mark, chosen not to know?

*A son: If "Rascal" was a girl, would Mark be disappointed? Mark's father would have what his wife called a "hissy fit." Calling Alabama to tell Mark's parents the news. "Gonna teach that boy to hoe garden and spit tobacco! Told coach—got him a new star coming up!"*

It was Mark's turn. "A gift," he said.

Tracy flashed him a smile, and then it was her turn.

"Faith," she said quickly, sure "faith" was the answer. It wasn't enough to want and to need. Even courage, even love, they weren't enough. Springboards, they got you going. Faith was the raft that kept you afloat.

Ending the session, the instructor reminded the group, "Don't get to the hospital too soon. When you can't walk, talk, or joke through a contraction, it's time to go."

On Christmas Eve, when she got out the tree ornaments, Tracy was feeling twinges. She handed a baby angel to Mark, who stood on the ladder, and felt a dull stabbing pain. She reached to hand him the crowning star and felt it again, low in her back.

"Mark!" she exclaimed, dropping the star.

He jumped down beside her, scanning her face. She reached for his hand.

"This is no joke," she gasped.

They were on their way.

Tracy crushed Mark's hand in the LDR (labor, delivery, recovery) room, trying to breathe when he coached her, trying to keep control. Mark, watching her face, pleaded with her to let him get help for the pain.

The nurse-instructor had explained medication was an option—a tool to be used if one chose. Tracy had chosen to deliver her baby drug-free. If she could tip the scales by a hair's breadth . . . if it would help . . . she would do it.

"Push—now!"

Tracy pushed—one last push, bearing down hard—and heard Mark say, "It's a girl!"

"A fine healthy girl!" the doctor said, holding the baby up.

Still holding Mark's hand, Tracy brought it to her cheek. As his face came down to hers, she could see his eyes, glistening above the mask.

"Merry Christmas, Mommy!"

Later that night, Tracy held Mark's hand in one of hers. The dark-haired infant, tucked into a red Christmas stocking, slept in her bassinet beside them.

"How did your father take the news?" she asked. "A Yankee *and* a girl!"

"Already enrolled her—Alabama, class of 2028. Now he's talking beauty queen!"

The baby whimpered, and Mark bent over her, kissing her forehead, inhaling the fresh, new smell of her. "I love you, Christmas-gift baby. You're what I always wanted. Little Rastine!"

*Rastine*. Knowing Mark, it was just the first in a series of love names. He would never run out. For Tracy, there would be only one name, now and forever. Pain, nurses, beauty, doctor, a gift of life, and love were all were part of their daughter's birth. A goal, inspired by courage, made real by faith. What else could they call her, but Faith?

# Now I Wonder . . .

by Leslie J. Wyatt

It was the week before Christmas, and snow lay sparkling white and deep as the fence posts. What a relief to my seven-year-old heart. I wasn't interested in playing in it so much as I was concerned that Santa's sled could arrive. Although I knew his reindeer could fly, surely a good three feet of snow guaranteed that if they got tired of being airborne, they could still reach our tiny house in the sagebrush.

Confident that a visit on Christmas Eve was assured, my siblings and I flitted from one activity to another, willing the time to pass. My mother, however, seemed quite busy in one corner of the dining room.

"What are you sewing, Mama?" I asked. "Doll clothes?"

She rolled her finger down the thread, knotting it at the end. "Mmmhmmm."

"For who?" I stared at the miniature bonnet taking shape in her hands. Gauzy lavender material lay like butterfly wings and matching satin ribbons trailed on her lap.

"For some little girls who need them."

My younger sister and I eyed each other. "We need them," we said, pressing closer.

Mama smiled, holding a bonnet up for us to see. "Well, I'm making these and leaving them for Santa Claus to pick up when he comes here. I'll write him a note so he knows to give them to some little girls he thinks might need them for their baby dolls."

"Oh." Disappointment mingled with admiration. My mother—my very own mother—was making doll clothes for Santa! I knew I should be happy for whatever child he would take the beautiful bonnets and dresses to, so I resigned myself as best I could.

Mama sewed in all her spare moments. My sister and I took to leaving our barely clothed dolls near her, hoping she'd notice how needy they were and put in a good word for us with Santa.

I'd never seen such pretty doll clothes: One set of lavender organdy containing bonnet, bloomers, and dress, complete with tiny puffed sleeves and pearl buttons, and an identical set in cotton-candy pink. I must have gazed at them a full ten minutes, visualizing how they would have looked on our dolls, thinking of how fun it would have been to dress them in such finery, and hoping that whoever got those clothes appreciated them as much as my sister and I would have.

Christmas Eve arrived at last. Mama helped us arrange a few cookies on a plate and set a glass of milk nearby in case Santa wanted a snack before he left for his next house. She even braved the cold, dark night outside to bring an armload of hay onto the porch in case Santa's reindeer wanted a snack.

There, beside the cookie plate, she placed her finished sewing with an accompanying note that we were not allowed to read.

"Santa can't come until you're all asleep," Mama reminded us, and we scurried to hide under our covers.

We were so full of anticipation that surely we could never relax long enough to drift off to dreamland. But of course we did, waking again in the wee hours of the morning and managing to rouse the rest of the sleeping house.

"Let's go see if Santa came," Mama said, and we blinked our way toward the glaring light of Daddy's movie camera. Only a few crumbs were left on the cookie plate, and the milk glass was empty.

"Well looky here," Daddy said, picking up a note written in big letters. "Thank you for the cookies and milk. Love, Santa."

A few scattered wisps of hay were all that the reindeer had left on the porch. Yes. Santa had definitely been here! But then I saw them, lavender and pink, laying there crisp and new, just like Mama had laid them out.

"Oh, Mama," I wailed. "Santa forgot to take the doll clothes!"

"Are you sure?" she asked.

"Yes, see?" I reached for the lavender set to show her. Just then I spied a note tucked under the pink bonnet.

"Dear children,
   Your mama asked me to give these to some little girls who needed them. I think your dollies could both use a new outfit.
                              Love, Santa."

Enveloped in wonder at what Santa Claus had done, we rushed to dress our "babies" in the new finery.

"Mama, look!" we squealed. "They fit perfectly. How did Santa know?"

Mama's eyes twinkled, but all she said was, "Now I wonder . . . "

Many Christmases have come and gone since that magic morning. One never passes but that I see again my mother's smile as she shared with us the enjoyment of the doll clothes she'd made "for some little girls who needed them" and wondered with us how "Santa" could have ever known the exact size that would fit our babies.

A Treasure Unspent

by Nan B. Clark

L ike thousands of other little girls in 1932, Mother had been duly warned that Santa wouldn't be leaving any presents that year.

It was the height of the Great Depression, a time of anxiety for most families. The familiar world had collapsed, taking with it the sense of security that all would be well. Even in a small farming town like Derry, New Hampshire, the reverberations from the stock market crash of 1929 continued to shake everyday existence into strange new forms and turn the simplest pleasures into unaffordable luxuries.

My grandfather was away in Wisconsin, working for a cousin who manufactured "billiard tables, of all things," as my grandmother said to anyone who asked, turning it into a pun. "I guess some folks still have deep pockets."

But Grandfather did mail money home every two weeks, and between that and my grandmother's pittance for taking in sewing, my mother was fed and clothed.

"You and I don't need presents to be happy," my grandmother started telling her at Thanksgiving. "Not as long as we have each other."

My mother pretended to agree, but inside, she was a grievously disappointed ten-year-old.

"No tinsel, no new ornaments, no strings of lights," Grandmother said. "Even so, Annie, I expect the spirit of Christmas won't be tarnished one whit," she added.

As for cookies, cakes, pies, and fudge, those luxuries were no longer coming out of my grandmother's kitchen—not even for the holidays. This Christmas Day they'd share a dessert of old-fashioned Indian pudding made with cornmeal and molasses, sweet enough for a child at any time but Christmas.

Although the holidays were much less commercialized back then, people of all ages still liked getting gifts and giving them. Mother cudgeled her brains trying to think of what she could make for Grandmother.

"I wasn't like her," Mother told me years later with a rueful laugh. "I couldn't sew a straight seam or knit a stitch without tangling one of the needles in my hair or poking the cat with it."

Finally, after many sleepless hours, she hit on the perfect gift. My mother would offer to clean the ashes out of the old black kitchen stove for a whole year, a chore she despised.

As for a tree, "Why chop down a poor little thing?" Grandmother said. "We'll pop up some popcorn, string it, and put it in our big tree out front for the birds to eat."

On Christmas Eve, the two went caroling, serenading the neighbors while a white, powdery snow swirled around them like the beneficent robes of an angel. That was wonderful enough, but early on Christmas morning, my mother opened her eyes to a miracle.

There on her little side table sat a perfect crèche, a manger, two funny-looking creatures that had to be a donkey and a cow, a tiny crib with a little figure in it, and two larger kneeling figures, Mary and Joseph.

The extraordinary thing, though, was that not only could the entire tableau fit on the palm of her hand, it was light as a feather. Every piece was composed of paper in the same blended shades of green, gray, and cream.

When she held the figures closer, my mother couldn't believe her eyes. They were made of money!

She saw that each dollar bill had been meticulously folded and creased. Although she hadn't yet learned the word "origami," my mother knew she was beholding something very special. Running to wake up my grandmother with the little paper manger scene held carefully in both hands, she wondered if a miracle had occurred for her mother, too. Naturally, in the way of all good stories that are cherished down the generations, it had. My grandfather was lying in the bed next to my grandmother.

"I hitchhiked some, and walked some, and took a train, and then a bus and then walked some more," my grandfather said as the three of them snuggled together. "And, you know how I covered the last few miles? I hitched a ride in a sleigh pulled by the slickest reindeer you ever did see."

My mother set up the manger scene on the quilt, so her folks could marvel at it, too. "So, Annie," her father asked, "how are you going to spend all that money?"

My mother's eyes widened. "Daddy, I'm never going to spend it. It's too precious."

He laughed and laughed, hugging her hard. "I guess that's a good lesson for these times," he finally said. "We all just have to remember that there really are things much more important than money."

My mother certainly did remember and taught me this lesson too. That is why, to this day, the same little manger scene rests gently on the mantel, gathering interest with every passing Christmas.

# Nothing Ever Happens in a Barn

by Suzanne Waring

*L*agging behind my mother on that cold December evening in the early 1950s, I looked up to see the stars as we walked to the car. Thousands of tiny white lights blinked brilliantly against the black sky. As a family, we often observed the Milky Way and constellations that adorned the night sky.

Getting into the car, I was startled when the door cracked shut in the silence of the still night. The cold scratched at my knees, and the plastic seat covers popped as we slid over them. Despite the temperature, the car roared to life. Before I knew it, the car lights were guiding me toward a task that I dreaded.

Christmas season had arrived, and Mother had recruited me to take packages of home-baked gifts up to neighbors' doors while she waited in the car to keep the motor running. Of her four children, I wondered why she had picked me for this miserable deed.

Up ahead, I spotted the lights of Mr. Green's milk barn. Those lights, and the far-away stars, stood out like welcoming ports in the evening darkness. Even though I sat next to my mother, I felt small and insignificant.

"Be certain to wish Mr. Green 'Happy Holidays' when you give him the fruit bread," she nudged. "He won't have any home-baked things, so he'll enjoy them."

Driving up to the milk barn, Mother coaxed me out of the car with still more coaching. I couldn't even answer her. How could I wish this stooped old man a good year? He had been an infrequent visitor to our house, and I hadn't ever gone out of my way to speak to him at community events.

In a few steps, I stood inside the milk barn. The sudden warmth washed over me, the smell of hay, manure, and milk rushing to my nostrils. A radio tinkled Christmas tunes softly in the background. Along with the gentle swooshing of the milking machines, I heard Mr. Green speak to one of the six Jersey cows eating hay from the stanchions.

"Hold still, Bess," he soothed. It wasn't *what* he said but *how* he said it that was at once comforting. Clutching the fruit bread wrapped in tin foil with a red bow stuck on top, I relaxed somewhat and glanced around the barn. But I was still annoyed that I had to be there in the first place. It looked like all the other milk barns in the neighborhood: uninspiring to a twelve-year-old girl. *This is Christmas,* I thought. *I should be having fun with the other kids! Why am I standing in this barn? Nothing ever happens in a barn!*

When Mr. Green stood up and saw me, the surprise on his face showed that he hadn't heard the door shut when I had come in and that he didn't have visitors to his barn often.

Faltering, he greeted me, "Hello . . . hello there." I realized that he didn't know what to say to me, and I certainly didn't know what to say to him.

As he stepped forward, I pushed the bread out in front of me and stammered, "My mother—well—this is for you. Merry Christmas, yes, my mother says have a good year." As this assortment of words tumbled out of me, I felt ridiculous. How could this bony old man in overalls have a good holiday? His wife was dead, he had no family, and he would have to milk those cows on Christmas just like on any other day of the year.

But it was obvious by his demeanor that I was wrong. He smiled at me as his veined wrinkled hand reached out to receive the loaf of bread.

"Your mother always brings me good things to eat. Tell her thanks."

The moment swept over me—his overwhelming gratitude for the insignificant gift, the warmth of the milk barn, my mother's pleasure of baking for her neighbors. Something in that moment changed me from the inside out. Returning Mr. Green's smile, I was glad I had come on this errand.

Many years have passed since that evening. I now live in a city where streetlights obliterate the stars on cold winter nights, and the closest milk barn is far away. But, I still have neighbors, and they are an important part of my life—and not just at Christmas. They have nourished me, and I hope I have nourished them.

As I look back on that Christmas, I realize my mother knew the moment was right for me to learn about the gifts one receives from giving to others. Today, so many years later, the vision of Mr. Green's barn and his soothing voice often come to me on chilly evenings. And when, in my vision, he accepts my mother's token gift and his face lights up with a smile, I find myself smiling back, just as I did that night so very long ago.

# A Bike for Christmas

by Wayne R. Wallace

ommy Miller wanted a red Schwinn Flyer bicycle more than he had ever wanted anything in all his ten years. He had seen a picture of one in a Sears & Roebuck Co. catalog, and that had started his dream. One Saturday morning, when he accompanied his dad into town, the dream became a tangible possibility. There, in the front window of Mr. Harris's Western Auto store, sat the most beautiful red Schwinn Flyer Tommy had ever seen. He stared at it longingly, then followed his dad inside. Tommy fingered the chrome fenders carefully as his father talked with Mr. Harris.

Tommy's dad was a rookie Oklahoma State Trooper on his first duty station in the small southern Oklahoma town of Marietta. The family of five had rented a tiny house just outside town. It was old and drafty, but it was all they could afford on the young patrolman's salary.

Though Tommy fell in love with the red metal dream in the window, he knew it could never be his. *Where would that kind of money come from?* Still, he couldn't get it out of his mind. That night, Tommy took a deep breath and approached his parents, almost ashamed to even ask.

"Dad, you know that red Schwinn Flyer we saw at Mr. Harris's store today?"

Ray Miller put down his paper. "Yes, it sure was a good-looking bike, son."

"Dad, I want that bike for Christmas," Tommy blurted. "I'll never ask for anything else, honest!"

"Tommy, I don't know . . . It's a lot of money, and we just don't have it right now," Mr. Miller explained.

"We'd love to get it for you if we could, sweetheart, but—we'll just have to see," Tommy's mother said as she pulled him close for a kiss. "Now off to bed, young man."

She turned to her husband as Tommy shut the bedroom door. "Ray, I'd sure like to get Tommy that bike. He works so hard around here, and he's done so well in school. Isn't there something we can do?"

"We'll work it out somehow," he said, reassuringly. "Maybe I can get a little off-duty security work. We should be able to save enough by Thanksgiving."

On Christmas Eve, Tommy and his brothers went to bed early. Tommy could think of nothing but the bike. It was on his mind every waking moment, and in his dreams, when he finally slept.

The next morning, the two younger boys ran into the family room and began opening packages. Tommy hung back. He knew that the bike cost a lot of money . . . money his parents didn't have. But when Tommy walked into the family room to join his brothers, there it was, waiting for him. It wasn't the one he'd seen in Mr. Harris's store. This one was better. It was gorgeous: a special edition Schwinn Flyer, much fancier than the one pictured in the catalogue. This one had white wall tires, chrome handlebars, and spoke wheels. It boasted a leather seat with springs and three gears! It was the best bike in the whole world, and now, it belonged to him!

Many years later, in 1978, Tommy, his wife, Kenna, and their young daughter, Stacey, were on their way to Dallas for the Christmas holiday. As they approached the Marietta exit, Tommy asked, "Kenna, do you mind if I stop and have a look at my old hometown? I'd like to see how it's changed."

"Not at all," Kenna replied. "It should be fun."

Main Street was decorated with garlands and lights, but Tommy noticed that most of the businesses he remembered had closed or had been bought by more modern franchises. When he realized that the old Western Auto Store was still open, he pulled up in front.

"Let's go in here," Tommy said. "Mr. Harris is an old friend."

As soon as they entered, Tommy spotted an old man standing behind the wooden counter and smiled. He would have known Mr. Harris anywhere, even after all these years.

"Hello, Mr. Harris," he said. "You probably don't remember me, but—"

"Tommy Miller!" Mr. Harris exclaimed. "Of course, I remember you! You used to come in here with your dad—you and your brothers."

The display of bicycles caught Stacey's eye, especially a small red tricycle, just her size. As Tommy watched his daughter's eyes light up, another young child came to mind. "I remember when my mom and dad got me my first bike for Christmas," he murmured.

Mr. Harris chuckled. "It came from my store. Christmas of '55. I remember it because I had sold the only red Schwinn I had just a couple of days before your dad came in. We had a blue one left, but it had to be red, he said. I told him I would order another one. It would be here in plenty of time for Christmas. Well, the bike didn't come in until the day before Christmas Eve. When he came to get it, we discovered it wasn't the same one he'd ordered, but a much more expensive model. He didn't have the money to pay the difference, and it was way too late to re-order. He was just about the nicest fellow I'd ever met, and he did a wonderful job with the highway patrol and all, so—I just made the balance on that fancy bike a Christmas gift from me. It moved him to tears . . . he thanked me over and over again."

"I know that meant a lot to him," Tommy replied quietly. "Dad never thought that he was anything special, but . . . he sure was to me."

"How is your dad, Tommy?" the storekeeper asked. "I haven't seen him in years—not since your family moved up north."

Tommy hesitated a moment. "He was killed in the line of duty three years ago," he said quietly. Tommy's gaze rested on the bicycles gleaming brightly in the window, a reminder of the sacrifices his parents had made for him so long ago. "He died on Christmas Eve."

Mr. Harris was deeply touched by Tommy's story. Sadly, he extended his hand for Tommy's farewell handshake. It was then that he noticed Tommy's daughter couldn't take her eyes off of the tricycle in his display case.

"Just a minute," he said. He walked to his display case and wheeled out the shiny, red tricycle. "Here you go, Miss Stacey—Merry Christmas."

"Oh, Mr. Harris, we can't possibly . . . " Tommy began, but the storekeeper waved him off with a grin.

"It's a gift for the little one, Tommy."

Mr. Harris chuckled as Stacey touched the red metal in awe and then climbed up onto the seat. He had seen that look before.

Glancing up at Tommy, he explained, "Some things never change . . . like kids and bikes at Christmas."

## Christmas Warmth

by Nancy Baker

**I** sat on the edge of the couch, huddled in my sleeping bag, inching as close as I dared to the wood-burning stove. I tossed another log in, but cold emanated from the un-insulated walls, from the bare floor, and from my sad, weary heart.

It was COLD! Bone-chilling, mind-numbing, all-encompassing cold. I had never been so cold. For three consecutive days, the temperature had dipped into the low teens at night and never rose above freezing during the day. This kind of weather was unheard of in Texas.

I pulled a quilt over my sleeping bag and curled into a tight ball. Closing my eyes against the frigid night air, I allowed my mind to drift back to my wonderful centrally heated home. I remembered how, with just a flick of the thermostat switch, warm air would rush in; how the fireplace had been more for show than heat; how you could have hot water in just a few seconds with a twist of the faucet. *Why, oh, why did we sell that lovely comfortable home?* Hot tears rolled down my cheeks, but my feet were still cold.

This was our dream—to live in the country. I had encouraged it, but now that we were living it, I found out it was no fun, especially since our cabin was unfinished. I had not anticipated all the changes this move would precipitate. I missed my children, my friends, my church, my job. I missed the convenience of being able to run to the corner store when I needed an ingredient for a recipe. I missed everything.

Now this unrelenting cold, which had frozen the pipes, making bathing next to impossible and cooking a nightmare. *Cooking!* My eyes flew open at the thought. Part of my family was coming tomorrow for Christmas. How on earth was I going to feed them?

Dawn brought sounds of my husband, Ted, moving about. Ted has always been one to sing or hum in the early morning. Today, his mood was a source of great irritation to me, and I dove deeper into my sleeping bag, not wanting to face the day or Ted's cheerfulness.

Heading outside, Ted hollered. "I've got to check on . . . " The end of his sentence was lost as the door slammed shut.

"Go," I mumbled. "Just leave me alone." It was not to be. Within minutes he was back.

"Honey, you've got to come see the waterfall. It's awesome."

He grabbed my coat and hat from the wall hook and tugged on my arm, literally dragging me from my nest near the stove.

"Alright!" I grumbled. "I'm coming."

I had to admit the sight was spectacular. The waterfall had frozen mid "fall." Icicles of all lengths reached toward the glazed surface of the pool below. The entire eight-foot width was covered with an icy fringe and the sun sent sparkling tiny rainbows from one icicle to another. It was a sight one doesn't see every day. As I observed the magnificence before me, some of the ice that had lodged in my soul seemed to melt.

We returned to the cabin just in time to answer the ringing phone. My younger son Pat was calling to say he and his wife, Maria, were on their way. Though I was glad to hear his voice, I wasn't so sure Christmas at our house was a good idea anymore.

"Oh son, are you sure you want to come?" I asked. "The weather is abominable."

"Mom," Pat's optimistic voice crackled over the phone line. "There'll be more of us—you know, more warm bodies. Can't miss Christmas with the family. We'll see you soon." Before I could utter another protest, the line went dead, and I felt my heart warm a little more.

As I stood musing on the subtle shift in my mood, I was startled by a knock on the door. Displaying a grin as wide as the Mississippi, my lifelong friend Barbara peered through the glass, clearly pleased with herself for surprising me. Craning her neck around Barbara was her mom, affectionately known as "Gau," who had taken me under her wing some twenty years ago when my own mom had died. Another shock awaited me when I threw open the door. Crouched to one side—so as not to be seen until the door swung wide—was my daughter, Laura.

"Surprise!" Laura yelled and grabbed me in a bear hug. It had been three months since I had last seen her and tears glistened as I held her tight.

"Laura! I thought you had to work."

"I pulled a double shift for two days so I could get time off." She backed away from me and wrinkled her nose. "Mama, you smell awful."

"Honey, I haven't been able to bathe. The pipes have been frozen, and we've had to carry water . . . "

"Well, we've got to do something about that," she declared, moving aside so Barbara could hug me.

"God, I've missed you," Barbara murmured. Then, she, too, stepped back sniffing. "Nancy, you stink!"

"I didn't expect you," I stammered. "The weather, the ice . . . "

"Couldn't let a little thing like ice stop us from spending time together at Christmas," Gau added as she blew me a kiss, wisely deciding to save the hug for later, as she set about making herself at home in my kitchen.

"I don't have much," I explained apologetically. "It's been so hard to get to the store with the ice."

Gau waved her hand airily. "We'll make do."

And as I watched her move through my kitchen with ease, I wiggled my toes. They were still numb, but my heart was thawing.

After a rather odd lunch of deviled eggs, fruitcake, olives, and coffee, Laura announced that it was time for my bath. In spite of myself, I laughed. How many times had I said those same words to her?

I smiled. "Honey, we can't waste our cooking water."

"Oh, yes, we can." She emphatically nodded her head, and I caught other nods with my peripheral vision. During my bath, my older son Vince arrived. I was squeaky clean by the time Pat and Maria pulled in.

"Time to get Christmas dinner on the stove," Gau directed.

My face flooded with color. "Gau," I whispered apologetically, "I don't have . . . "

"Nonsense! I taught you to stock your pantry. We'll find something."

Our Christmas dinner that year consisted of Dinty Moore stew and canned biscuits, but I never enjoyed a meal more. As I listened to the banter around the table, I realized this coldest of cold Christmases was very warm indeed.

# Christmas Card from My Sister

### by Joan Rawlins Biggar Husby
Robe, Washington

My sister's Christmas card painting takes my breath away . . . not the skill or the composition or the color, though all three are there.

Here I sit—sixty years distant from the events pictured—and gaze at her watercolor remembrance. Memories and emotions swirl. It's like a scene in a snow globe. Flakes settle deep on roof and evergreens and drape a mantle of white over Green Mountain. The sky over all is purple and black.

Our little house nestles in the woods beneath the mountain, and lamplight warms the windows. Out front, children play. I'm a child again . . . the tallest one with yellow hair. Sister Lois, who grew up to paint the picture, helps me pat our snowman into shape. I can feel the chill of ice melting through my hand-knit mittens, stiffening my fingers. Our mischievous middle sibling, Billy, pushes a snowball bigger than he is. Little sister Patty, down on her knees, tries to roll a snowball, too, and David, the smallest child, stamps his feet and crows with delight.

Our toes grow numb in rubber galoshes, but we scarcely notice. Our shouts and laughter ring in the clean air. No other noise disturbs the silence because the road is buried. Until the big yellow plow scrapes its way from town, we are the only people in the world. Loggers, like our father, can't get into the woods, and if any neighbors are out and about, snow muffles their sounds.

Soon, Daddy will come out to shovel the steps and the path to the house. Then he will begin the long task of clearing the driveway, taking care to avoid our snow art. We will clamor for turns at the shovel and get in his way. We are safe and contained—a family—and the joy of it makes us giddy.

As the morning warms or if a breeze comes up, branches spring free of their loads, sending miniature avalanches cascading to the ground. When we finish our snowmen, we tramp a circle in the unbroken white that blankets the garden. We persuade Daddy to stop shoveling long enough to join us for a game of fox and geese.

Behind the lighted window, Mama is baking bread in the old woodstove oven. The fragrance leaks out to mingle with the scent of evergreens. When she calls us for lunch, we come in breathless and shed wet wraps. We line five pairs of galoshes along the wall in the covered porch, five jackets and hats on hooks.

"Hang your mittens on the line behind the stove," she reminds us with a smile before turning back to flip rounds of bread dough in the frying pan.

Rosy-cheeked, with snowflakes melting in our hair, we crowd around the table while the child whose turn it is recites, "Come, Lord Jesus, be our guest . . . ." Then we pile our plates with hot, crispy dough babies and pour on the syrup.

Outside, the snow tumbles from the trees and settles onto the ground. The plow growls by, pushing up a berm of chunks along one edge of the road. When it comes back, heaping up the other embankment, Daddy will dig through the wall so the car can leave the driveway. But at the moment, we're busy filling our tummies so we can go out again.

The original of my sister's painting now hangs framed above our ninety-six-year-old mother's bed. Lois wrote the name of each child on the glass, but Mama has gone where memories can't follow. The love that made a snug home for us and gave us fried dough babies on a wintry afternoon remains, however. When her aging children come to visit, it shows in the smile that hasn't changed for sixty years.

# Spotlight on Robe, Washington

## Town Facts

**Population:** 260
**First incorporated:** The community
remains unincorporated.
**Location:** Robe is located in prime recreational country
about fifty miles northeast of Seattle, Washington,
in the Cascade Mountains. It is a wonderful place to live,
not only because of the surrounding mountains, the tall
timber, and the river running through it, but also
because of its unique history.

## The History of Robe

The valley where the South Fork of the Stillaguamish River flows once rang with clanging axes, donkey whistles, and shouts of "*timber!*" accompanied by the screech of sawmills and the voices of homesteaders. The whistles of railroad trains echoed from the wild peaks surrounding the Monte Cristo mines, far up the valley—all the way to the new industrial city, Everett, on Puget Sound. The trains carried ore from rich deposits of gold and other minerals discovered in 1889. The Stillaguamish Indians (River People) lived along the lower reaches of the river long before the miners, loggers, and settlers arrived.

Though the character was and is distinctly rural, in the '40s and '50s, the Robe community boasted a few city amenities, including Green Gables—a gas-station/grocery store, which was built in 1936. The community also had a polling place in the old schoolhouse and a post office. The post office operated out of Susie Buchanan's front room. Additionally, Susie started the Mountain View Inn restaurant, which later added a lounge, a mini mart, and a motel. The ranger station at Verlot, also built in 1936, still stands guard over the Mt. Baker–Snoqualmie National Forest, campgrounds, and mountain trails. The Civilian Conservation Corps built the ranger station and many of the campgrounds and trails during the Depression. For a long time afterward, the Forest Service was a dependable employer of young locals.

## Robe Is Built, Abandoned, and Resurrected

The railroad along the river and the overland wagon road brought the first settlers to the valley, including pioneer Wirt Robe, whom the town was named after.

When Robe became a settlement in 1910, it had a population of 150 and contained one sawmill, one planing mill, and one shingle mill, as well as one hotel, one general store, and the post office. Unfortunately—despite local warnings that summer's chuckling trout stream became a roaring torrent during winter storms—the East Coast engineers insisted on building the railroad along the river. They drilled six tunnels through the canyon, forty feet above the river, but after repeated flooding destroyed tunnels and bridges, the railroad was finally abandoned, and so was the town.

Other settlements such as Turlo and Verlot dotted the valley at Gold Basin. As logging activity moved farther into the mountains and mining activity at the now–ghost towns of Monte Cristo and Silverton ceased, the valley settlements lost their individual character. Gradually, the communities expanded, filling in the several miles along the Mountain Loop Highway. They became known as either Robe—in honor of the old town on one end—or Verlot, the settlement at the other end of the stretch. Today, the area is generally called Robe Valley.

These days, children still ride buses nine miles (or more, depending upon where their families live) to school in Granite Falls, which is the closest town. The last country school building stood for a number of years after closure, and then it was used as a community center. At one time, this building also served as a place for neighborhood dances and community potlucks and parties. The old school building is where grownups voted in their favorite politicians and where children met for Sunday school every Sunday afternoon. In the winter, fathers took turns building the fire in the big round cast iron heater, and in the summer, after classes, families often met to play baseball in a clearing at Gold Basin campground.

## Famous People

From time to time, famous people have visited Robe to enjoy the fabulous scenery. One who stayed was Kenneth Callahan, a well-known artist and a founder of the "Northwest School" of painting. With his wife, Margaret Bundy, he built a cabin on 145 acres that they bought in 1946 in a secluded spot near the old town of Robe. After 1952, the widely traveled Callahan spent summers painting and selling paintings from this cabin. Fire destroyed the cabin and many paintings in 1963, and Callahan died in 1986.

Most of the people who live in Robe Valley tend to be the kind of folks Norman Rockwell immortalized in his paintings: common, decent, everyday people who work hard and are good neighbors to each other and to those who come to enjoy their community.

## Robe Today

Very little logging takes place around the Robe Valley today. Most people drive to jobs in Everett or Seattle and shop or attend church in the larger towns. But the community is flourishing. Green Gables and the Mountain View Inn are still in business, serving the hordes of vacationers who drive through the valley along the Mountain Loop Highway, camp in the parks beside the river, and fish or hike the popular mountain trails.

The Sainted Arm of the Holiday

by Renee Willa Hixson

It was Christmas Eve day, and we were broke. Flat broke. The sainted arm of the holiday season would never find us so far up in the Ozark foothills. We were just one woman and her six children, sequestered in a tiny summer cabin that teetered on the slopes of Chicken Creek, Oklahoma. Living quarters consisted of one room, separated into two by bed sheets hung from the ceiling. Food was whatever Mom could buy at the tiny neighborhood store. The only entertainment was to run around the cabin in a rousing game of tag.

"Go outside and play!" Mom sputtered as my younger brother and sister collided in front of her where she was sweeping. In the next instant, we all were promptly banished to the cold outdoors.

My brother and I ran toward the hard clay road in front of our cabin where a battered round cylinder awaited—our own private amusement ride. Eagerly, I wedged myself into the cylinder and tensed for the ride that would take me winding down the hill from our driveway.

"Ready?" Jerry cried. Without waiting for a reply, he pushed.

*Whump! Bang!* The barrel bounced and ricocheted as gravity pulled it downward. Weaving from side to side, it bounced off rocks embedded in the frozen ground. With a final clang, the barrel smacked a solid clump of icy snow, flew up into the air, and then crashed in the ditch.

I crawled out of the barrel, slowly. My skin quivered and my heart pounded as if I was still in flight. Slightly dazed, I turned when I heard a car honk. Before I could move out of the way, an immaculate gray sedan pulled up beside me.

"Get away from the road," Grandpa barked. "Before you get killed!" Without another word, he eased his vehicle up the incline toward the cabin. I took off running so that I could reach the cabin before he did. Quickly, I crawled through a hole in the lattice around the bottom of the porch and flopped onto the cold hard ground. Grandpa was a busy man with summer cabins and other investments—he didn't have time to visit in the middle of the day! Whatever it was he needed to say to my mom must be important.

Grandpa's engine purred to a stop beside the porch. "Norma Jean!" He called as he climbed out of the car, "Are you home?"

Above me, a screen door slammed, and footsteps sounded as Mom stepped from the house.

"Just come to remind you about Christmas dinner tomorrow," Grandpa said without waiting for Mom's greeting. "Grandma's been cooking all day."

I peeked out from my hiding place as Grandpa spoke. He crossed his arms and leaned against the cold metal of his car. "By the way, did that husband of yours get a job yet? It's been over a month since he went south to find one. Should a' kept the one he had."

For a moment, it was very quiet on that weathered front porch. So quiet, I could hear the sound of the winter wind rustling the bare branches of the trees clustered around the cabin.

When Mom finally spoke her voice was clear and her tone firm. "Dad, I told you. Roy had to leave his work for ethical reasons."

Grandpa shook his head and pulled out his wallet.

"It's okay, Dad," Mom said as she refused his money. "Roy will be home for Christmas."

"Don't hold your breath," Grandpa muttered as he slid his wallet back into his pocket. "The weather is bad on the roads between here and Texas. He'll be lucky to make it for New Year's."

*Dad? Not home for Christmas?* My eyes were almost too full of tears to witness Grandpa handing Mom a bag of Christmas candy canes through his car window. I waited until he left, then I slithered out from my cold dark hideout like a whipped puppy. Mom was at the stove stirring a pot of creamy potato soup when I walked inside.

"Hey!" She said and quickly wiped her hands on her faded Christmas apron so she could give me a hug. "Tears on a muddy face? You been under the porch listening to me and Grandpa?"

I nodded my head as my lower lip quivered.

Mom put her arm around me. "Hey," she said gently, "Grandpa's just worried about his youngest daughter and her herd of kids. He's wasting his time. I know your dad too well."

That night, I lay in bed unable to sleep. In just a few hours it would be Christmas Eve. *What if Dad didn't make it back? What if Grandpa was right?* Finally, I slipped out of bed and crawled to the curtain that separated our sleeping room from the living area, and sprawled out on the cold wooden floor to watch Mom. She sat at the kitchen table and worked tirelessly with a bunch of wooden thread spools. A hammer and various bright colored odds and ends lay in front of her on the table as she made toys. A small car made with wheels from thread spools. A soft cotton doll and a yellow-stitched dress. A game made of brightly painted pieces of wood. I watched Mom make Christmas presents, until sleep finally claimed me.

A few hours later, I was awakened by a loud noise. I sat up on the cold wooden floor and looked around. The door to the cabin opened slowly and a dark form stepped inside and grabbed my mom!

"Dad," I squealed as I scrabbled to my feet. "You're home!"

My yells woke my brothers and sisters. They tumbled from behind the curtain and threw themselves at Dad. Smiling, Mom led him to his big brown vinyl easy chair. As Dad told us about his new job down in Texas, Mom walked to the stove and heated up milk for hot chocolate. As she stirred the milky substance, Mom rubbed her bleary eyes and smiled. We were broke. Flat broke. Yet, somehow the sainted arm of Christmas had found us after all.

A Christmas to Cherish

by Terri Meehan

𝓘 will never forget Christmas the year I was seven years old.

In the 1950s, my anticipation of the holiday season usually began around mid-August. Coincidentally, that was the same time the Sears, Roebuck & Company toy catalog showed up in our mailbox. My two brothers and I could not contain our excitement as we chose the toys we hoped to receive that year. Top on my list was the Shirley Temple doll dressed in a white dress with red polka dots. I tore the page from the catalog and gave it to my dad when he asked me what I wanted for Christmas. I was certain that I would get my wish since neither my parents nor Santa wished to see me disappointed.

It seems like the passage of time takes forever when you're a kid waiting for the big day to arrive. To try and abate my enthusiasm, I started decorating my bedroom with green construction paper Christmas trees. I will never forget that mild mid-November evening when I heard my dad arrive home from work. I stopped what I was doing, immediately, and dashed to the kitchen to greet him. Something in his expression made me stop before throwing myself into his arms.

Dad had just been to the hospital to visit Grandpa, who had been undergoing tests since September. The news was not good.

"Does that mean Gramps won't be home for Christmas?" I asked. "I don't know," Dad replied. I went back to my bedroom and closed the door behind me. I didn't feel like decorating if Grandpa would not be home for Christmas.

The following week Grandma got a call from the hospital. Grandpa would be discharged on Christmas Eve, but he'd have to return on December 26. That was good news for all of us.

A few days before Dad went to get Grandpa, Grandma asked him if he would climb into the attic to bring down the outdoor decorations. I knew the exact ones she was referring to. They were part of the family's cherished Christmas heirlooms—the ones Grandpa could never part with. When Dad pulled down the attic steps, I followed close behind. It was like walking into Aladdin's cave filled with a cornucopia of treasures! My curiosity was in full gear as I snooped through boxes while Dad uncovered the four wooden choirboys.

I helped Dad carry the decorations downstairs and noticed how tarnished and yellow the choirboys' white robes had become. Dad told me the paint had discolored because the decorations were so old. The choirboys had been part of the family since my grandparents got married more than fifty years ago. But tarnished or not, they were Grandpa's pride and joy. Dad set two of them on each side of the porch. Once the spotlights were switched on, the display radiated with a golden, angelic sheen. Each night, I stood at the picture window in our house across the road and admired the view.

When Christmas Eve finally arrived, I went with my dad to the hospital to bring Grandpa home. As we pulled into Grandpa's driveway, I had to admit the staging could not have been more perfect. The full moon shining on the newly fallen snow created a perfect backdrop for Grandpa's beloved choirboys.

As Grandpa's eyes welled up with tears, he whispered. "This is the best gift ever."

I leaned forward and touched his arm. "For me too," I replied. And even today, as I remember how wonderful it felt on Christmas morning to hold my Shirley Temple doll in my arms, I know there will never be anything quite as wonderful as having shared that first and last glimpse of Christmas splendor with my grandpa.

## A Memorable Family Gathering

by Bob Rose

It was 1970—Christmas morning—the first Christmas in my parents' new home, and I was home from my first year at college. Mom's sister, Aunt Lil, and her husband, Bob, joined our family as we lounged lazily in the comfort of pajamas and bathrobes. I recall how the fire crackled in the fireplace and how the smells of the forthcoming Christmas dinner cooking in the kitchen assailed our senses. Lights twinkled on the tree; torn wrapping paper cluttered the floor; light, reflecting from the fresh-fallen snow, poured in through the floor-to-ceiling windows.

Suddenly, Mom jumped up and ran from the room. She returned minutes later, carrying two more presents.

Living in rural Wyoming, far from malls and shopping centers, Mom made each shopping trip count. No matter what time of year, if she spotted a potential gift, she bought it, especially if it happened to be on sale. She took it home, wrapped it, and stashed it away for Christmas. She usually tagged the gifts before putting them away—usually.

"I almost forgot about these two," she said. "And I see that I forgot to put tags on them, so I hope this is right," she added as she handed one gift to my father and the other to my fourteen-year-old sister.

My dad was a powerful man in his prime. He had developed great strength from working in the family blacksmith shop. Still, he had the heart of a child. He ripped away the wrapping and removed the contents of the box. He held the purple nightshirt—appliquéd with an owl—against his chest.

He sighed. "I certainly hope this isn't for me."

Everyone else in the room burst out in laughter. Mom, who seldom allowed others to see her emotions, laughed hardest of all. Her glee soon turned to giggles, which played against Aunt Lil's own developing hysteria. They both struggled to control themselves, but then one would catch the other's eye, and it would begin anew. Their giggling became infectious. Soon, even my father began to see the humor in the situation.

Ours had never been a demonstrative family. Mom's immigrant family simply did not believe in showing emotion, and Dad grew up in the role of the family black sheep. His actions frequently brought ridicule, so he learned to keep everything inside. My sister and I entered the family late in their lives, as waiting lists for adoption were long, and the wait interminable. By the time I had arrived, and my sister, five years later, Mom and Dad were used to order, peace, and quiet. They expected us to keep things that way. We were not a family known for creating warm, fuzzy memories, until that Christmas.

Mom and her sister gave into their feelings. Even Dad laid aside the fear of being mocked and enjoyed a day of laughing along.

Today, only my sister and I remain from the group that was there that day, but I can still see the expression on Dad's face when he first saw the nightshirt. Mom and Aunt Lil's giggles still echo through my mind's ear.

I now have children and grandchildren of my own, and our gatherings on Christmas morning echo with laughter. But once the presents are opened, the children begin to play with their new treasures, and the noise dies down, I close my eyes, and step back in time, and I laugh all over again.

# A Basket of Straw

## by Wanda Winters-Gutierrez

Like most Christian families raising small children, my husband and I were concerned about retaining the true meaning of Christmas. And, like most families, we found it difficult. Our four children had a pastor-daddy and a writer-mommy—our home life was not what one would call sedate. In fact, one could call it wild.

Around Christmas, our already intense living style picked up speed until we were spinning in circles, hardly knowing what to do next, much less having time to think about the Prince of Peace. I had come to the conclusion that the true meaning of Christmas would have to wait until I found out the true meaning of sanity.

But, knowing I needed to find a way to enrich this holy time for my children, I began to search for ideas. A number of options came to mind. Unfortunately, the Advent calendar—with its little pockets stuffed with tiny sweet treats to be opened each day before Christmas—didn't work because two-year-old Chrissie Paul got up early. Two days into our new tradition, he decided to eat the whole month's worth of treats—all before breakfast.

Undaunted, we tried the Advent wreath. I loved the incredibly beautiful and romantic dream of a family gathering for a few minutes on the four Sundays before Christmas to hear the immortal story about a baby who came to fill the world with love. I envisioned our four children taking turns lighting the Advent candles. In their starry eyes, I just knew I would see the wonder the angels sang about.

In reality, we had to replace the candles a few times because the idea of lighting just one candle a week for only a few minutes didn't go over well. The baby thought he needed to light a candle every time anybody else did, and the girls thought if there was a candle around it ought to be on the table and lit every time we ate. The whole concept went right over their heads.

Then there was the tradition of the basket of straw. This one worked pretty well and actually touched the very heart of what we wanted to do during the Christmas season. Above all, we wanted to remind ourselves that the baby born to Mary that first Christmas came down from heaven to help us become better people and that we have a solemn responsibility to share that love with others in real ways.

We found a basket, wrapped a small doll in swaddling clothes, and placed soft fragrant straw nearby. The idea was to make a soft bed for Baby Jesus before Christmas Eve. The catch was that you could put a piece of straw into the basket only if you had done a loving deed for another or attitude toward another. These deeds and attitudes had to come from a pure heart.

At the same time, when one of us acted unkindly, caused pain to another or was unfair, he/she had to remove straw from the basket. This reminded us in a graphic way that our actions hurt our Lord, just as laying Baby Jesus in a bed void of hay would have bruised him.

Any number of actions helped fill the manger. Lisa, our oldest, was allowed to put in a few straws when she helped her sister finish her work without complaining. Sherry, our second daughter, put in a hefty portion the day she found her room in total disarray caused by her little brother. She handled it by saying, "Mikie, what am I going to do with you? Come help Sissie clean this up." The little fellows sometimes put their straw in for refraining from punching a brother or sister when said brother or sister clearly deserved punching. Even Mom and Dad participated in the straw tradition.

There were also sad times. When the action of one of our family members was not becoming to a child of God, we walked to the basket and took out five or six straws. Then we took a few moments to ask forgiveness for our behavior. Each time we vowed to do better.

The first year we tried this was the year I got in big trouble and had occasion to think deeply about the last aspect of our new tradition. It was the fourth week in Advent—I was totally exhausted. There had been too many meetings, too many late nights, and too many questions from too many little people.

I was trying to nap before dinner, but the noise coming from my troops downstairs had steadily mounted until it reached a dull roar. In a fit of anger, I forgot all about being like a child of God.

"What is the matter with you kids?" I yelled. "Can't you see I'm trying to rest?" Wide-eyed children looked back at me, but I continued my tirade. I was well into my screaming fit when I happened to glance at the basket of straw. When I looked back at my children, three sets of brown eyes and one set of blue nailed me to the wall. Nobody said a word. They didn't have to; my soul ached.

In a voice filled with remorse, I whispered, "I am so sorry."

With shaky steps, I walked to the basket, my young children walking beside me as I had walked beside them when they had done wrong. As I reached down and picked up a handful of straw, the tears began pouring down my face. In anguish, I buried my face in the straw and sobbed my heart out. And then the most miraculous thing happened. The little hands of my children reached out to me, forgivingly.

I gathered them close. Our tears mingled and fell into the manger, and together we prayed for a mommy who was still learning to practice what she preached—still learning what it meant to be a child of God.

## Mama's Gift

by Karen Wilson

ama was ninety-one years young the year she passed away. I say "young" because that's what she surely was. She had always maintained a spirit of joy and determination about her, despite her circumstances. She could see the good in all and lived her entire life with perseverance and diligence. She was full of intelligence and wit and had an endless supply of humor. She could find something funny in just about every situation.

Not surprisingly, her favorite holiday was Christmas. How she loved having all the children and grandchildren and great-grandchildren over to her home every Christmas Eve. There was always a ton of presents, plenty of food to eat, Christmas skits to perform, songs to be sung, and poems to be recited. And, she always had gifts for everyone.

I lived about 500 miles away from my mom, and since Dad had passed away two years previously, I tried to call her on the telephone about once a week to see how she was getting along. Though she was always happy to hear by voice, on one particular phone call in February, she could hardly contain her excitement. She'd already decided what she was going to give me for Christmas that year.

Because her gifts were usually something handmade, she teased me mercilessly about the gift, trying to get me to guess what it was, yet never giving me the slightest clue about it.

Three months later, the day before Mother's Day, Mama died of a heart attack. As the months passed, I forgot about the Christmas gift. But, as Christmas approached that year, I again remembered her excitement and wondered what the gift could have been. All her personal effects had been dispersed by that time, and I figured I'd never know.

Then a miracle occurred.

A few days before Christmas, there was a knock at the door. It was the UPS man. To my surprise, he was there to deliver a very large package that was addressed to me. Though I had no idea what it was, or who had sent it, I was excited to be receiving such a big box—surely it was a Christmas gift. When I opened the box, I was equally surprised to find two charming snowmen: Mr. and Mrs. Snowman. I was thrilled! They were large, soft, and huggable.

I laughed out loud in delight and placed the snowmen on the counter to admire them. Then I picked up the note that accompanied the gift. In an instant, my laughter turned into great gushing sobs that were borne of gratitude and thankfulness. Though Mama hadn't given in and told me what the gift she was making me for Christmas had been, she apparently had mentioned it to a close family friend. And, when at the time of Mama's passing, seeing that the snowmen were not finished, this friend—as a labor of love to both me and my mother—had not only finished the project, but had also remembered to send the gift to me in time for Christmas.

I hugged the stuffed snowmen tightly and let the tears flow down my cheeks unchecked. It was my first Christmas without Mama, but this gift helped bring her back home for Christmas one more time.

Three Giant Wise Men

by Nancy Jo Eckerson

At age five, and less than four feet tall, I was devoted to my giant of a dad. I followed him like a shadow wherever he went.

When my parents decided to put an addition on our house, I followed Dad around, my apron pockets filled with nails, ready to help him. As the village building inspector, one of his many part-time jobs, he would allow me to come along for the ride while he inspected new building sites. That was a very special time for Dad and me. I would consult with him about the events of the day at school or pose my endless questions about life. We would stop at the bakery and sneak a couple of doughnuts, just before dinner, hiding the wrappers under the car seat, to not alert my mom. We shared great secrets like that.

I was particularly attached to his hip every Christmas. In my tiny town of 3,500, our Christmas was a community-wide event. All the churches, houses, and municipal buildings were decked out in pine, holly, and colored lights. Main Street glowed with wreaths of colored bulbs centered between snow-topped, evergreen swags that swooped across every block.

Each Christmas season, the adults all seemed just a little nicer and more patient than usual with us kids. I would notice that the old men, who were normally gruff, adopted a softer tone. A sparkle shone, even in *their* weary eyes, at that time of year.

The very best part of the Christmas anticipation came from our church activities. There were scrumptious dinners and tree-decorating parties in the fellowship hall with friends and family. When it came time for caroling door-to-door, even the kids were allowed to go, meeting at the church for hot chocolate after the singing. Some evenings, we would carpool to carol at nursing homes or for shut-ins who lived far from the church. Touring the countryside in Dad's big, black '55 Buick, viewing the houses lit up with lights, was a favorite seasonal activity.

Probably one of the most important events at Christmastime, though, was the Christmas Eve service. I can remember the feeling of awe as we approached the church, and I looked up and saw the huge wreath, with its shiny red bow, that covered the entire front of the building. Inside, the sanctuary glowed with candlelight. In one corner was a gigantic tree, with shining lights, that held gold and glass ornaments.

This was a very solemn time. A lot was riding on just how well a child could sit still during that service. One slip and Santa would surely take one of your major gifts away before the next morning. This was a time, above all others, to be on your best behavior.

I can still feel the amazement vibrating through me as I sat in that huge church pew, my short little legs pointed straight out to the hymnal rack, anticipating what was to come. My only regret each year was that, at the very same time as the whole Christmas pageant buildup was going on, my dad would always be called away. I ached to have him witness this grand procession. The three kings of "Orientar" would always show up to announce the coming birth of the star named Jesus, and Dad would always be gone.

Year after year, it was always the same. Everyone grew silent as the stately footsteps sounded in the hallway. You could have heard a pin drop, and not one pair of little black patent-leather shoes made a sound. Suddenly, the double doors would burst open and in would walk the kings' servant. He would clear the way for their majesties to enter the sanctuary. It was a sight to behold. The deep burgundy robes with gold trim were so very regal, and the crowns, laden with jewels, sparkled so brightly you could barely keep your eyes on them. The Three Giant Wise Men, as they were called, would slowly walk down the aisle in a most majestic manner. One king was Frank, and the other two had odd names—Incense and Myrrh.

These kings were on their way to Jerusalem, which was even farther away than Buffalo, I was told. As always, they would stop by our church every Christmas to share some of the baby Jesus' gifts. That is why I came to love the baby Jesus. Anyone who would share his treasure of gold was someone I felt safe with, someone I would remain loyal to for life. And this was not your ordinary gold; this was precious, chocolate-filled coinage, even more valuable than the real thing!

The kings would proceed to the altar and then, one at a time, we children were expected to go forth and kneel at the rail to receive one of Jesus' red plastic net stockings full of treats. This was my time to shine, as each year the kings would shift positions so that Myrrh, with his long gray beard, would always be the one to give me my stocking. I felt very special. Oh, how I wished my dad could have been there!

by Ray Wong
Ridgecrest, California

$\mathcal{G}$ don't know why I went back to Ridgecrest on Christmas. I had been feeling down, kind of empty, as if I didn't belong anywhere. Something—a yearning—tugged at me to return to the small, insignificant California desert town where my stepfather had been stationed in the Navy.

I drove the rental car into the parking lot at Pierce Elementary and felt a flood of emotions. I got out of the car and slowly walked along the dirt field where we used to play marbles, letting the memories flow over me. I imagined a little boy tossing his marble onto the sand, and the two of us taking turns trying to hit the other's marble. The trick was to throw hard enough so that if I missed, my opponent wouldn't have an easy shot. I didn't want to throw too hard, though, or else the marbles might chip upon contact. A chipped marble was practically worthless.

I continued to walk amid the symbols of my past. At the climbing ropes, I'd lost my favorite marble—a green purey—to that freckle-faced boy named Mike Waters. I could still recall my shock, then disappointment, when his red purey struck my green one. I just stood and watched him slip my marble into his pocket.

When I reached the blacktop, I stepped onto the tar and other memories assailed me: kids skirting in every direction, the chanting "Not it! Not it!" at the start of freeze tag, a jump rope hitting the ground, chortling laughter, a high-pitched voice, "Nah uh, you didn't get me—you didn't!"

At the far end of the blacktop, two groups of children played basketball. To the right, girls engaged in hopscotch, their ponytails and braids swishing as they skipped and jumped. On the four-square courts, I heard the loud argument about "holdsies" or "double bouncies." A line of impatient boys and girls waiting their turn exhorted the players to hurry up. In the big circles at the middle of the blacktop, kids played dodge ball. We weren't supposed to throw above the waist, but it seemed as if somebody was always getting thumped in the head.

Then I saw the tetherball pole. I always missed the tetherball, and before I knew it, the ball would be wrapped around the pole on my side. After I got hit in the face by the tetherball, I never played it again.

I thought about the wheelie contests after school with Mark Lyons and Antonio Dobbins. How I relished racing across the blacktop on my green Huffy, the wind licking my face, my hands clenching the waffle handle grips as I popped my best wheelies.

Heading toward the classrooms, I admired the snowflakes and shiny-nosed reindeer, snowmen in top hats and scarves, and glittering Christmas trees that decorated the windows. Once inside the building, I found the way to my second-grade classroom, where a huge Santa waved cheerfully at the door.

I peeked through a window and spotted a big, round, black clock with a white face. A red second hand circled the black numbers. Four rows of desks faced a long, green chalkboard, and alphabet cards displaying capital and lowercase letters adorned the walls.

I remembered how my second-grade teacher, Mrs. Maine, with her short, puffy red hair and thick brown glasses, danced across the room handing out happy faces. Students who came in quietly after recess received a happy face, and at the end of the week, prizes were awarded for the happiest faces.

Mrs. Maine was the only teacher who ever read to us after lunch. That year, she read *Charlotte's Web*. She only read for about fifteen minutes a day, but it sure made for an easier transition to spelling. I dreaded spelling, but somehow, listening to her read soothed me.

Mrs. Maine had a clear firm voice that drew us in. Her eyes grew big, and she made sweeping arcs with her arms to show us the action. A collective groan rose from the class at the end of each reading period.

That winter, we made clay Christmas ornaments. Other kids molded Santas and elves out of red and green clay. I don't know why I chose to make a brown house with yellow windows. The other kids teased me—a brown house with yellow windows had nothing to do with Christmas. Mrs. Maine put a stop to the laughing. She said Christmas could be symbolized in many ways. Then she came over and knelt beside me.

She put her hand on my shoulder and said, "Raymond, I really like the house you made. I can tell it's a very special house." I don't know if I've ever had a better feeling than when she smiled at me just then.

That was the best school year I ever had. We moved the next summer, and I started another school. A kid named Jimmy told me there was no such thing as a real Santa Claus. The new teacher didn't pass out happy faces, and she didn't read to us after lunch.

I took one long last look into the classroom window. On the wall next to the chalkboard, a huge, green calendar showed a boy and a girl, in snowcaps and mittens, building a snowman. Candy canes marked off the days of the year. A big, white glowing star shone on the 25th.

I smiled and turned slowly from the classroom. I wandered back outside and walked to the climbing ropes, took off my shoes and unfastened the cuffs of my long-sleeved shirt. I rolled the sleeves up and began climbing. At the very top, I pulled my legs over the support bar, and holding on with the back of my knees, I dangled upside down. My keys, some change, my wallet, and a half-opened roll of cough drops fell to the sand. It didn't seem to matter.

I looked over at the school and saw the orange sky on the ground. Then I gazed up at my old classroom. It had taken the place of the sky.

# Spotlight on Ridgecrest, California

## Town Facts

**Population:** 26,000
**First incorporated:** 1963
**Original name:** Crumville
**Location:** Ridgecrest, the only incorporated community in the Indian Wells Valley, lies in the Mojave Desert and covers approximately 13,000 acres. It is east of the Sierra Nevada Mountains and west of Death Valley National Park and is bordered by three other mountain ranges, the Cosos, Argus Range, and El Paso Mountains. Ridgecrest neighbors the counties of Bakersfield and San Bernardino.

## Industry

Industry and business in Ridgecrest are varied and include the Naval Air Weapons Station China Lake (defense), Searles Valley Minerals (mining of soda ash products), and Sierra Sands Unified School District (education). Additionally, Matrix Motor Company Inc., founded in 1995 in California, currently is headquartered in Ridgecrest. The business operates a manufacturing and sales facility of race cars and parts.

## From Crumville to Ridgecrest

In 1912, a family with the surname of Robertson developed a homestead on the land in the area now known as Ridgecrest. John McNeil and his wife, store owners in the town of Inyokern, purchased property there to start a dairy and then sold it to Robert Crum, who named his settlement,

"Crumville." Local citizens later wanted to call the town Sierra View, but the post office indicated California already had many "Sierras." The town took a vote on its new name, and "Ridgecrest" won by one vote.

Over the years, growth has been continual. Since the early 1940s, when the Naval Ordinance Test Station (NOTS)—now known as China Lake Naval Air Warfare Center—was established by the Navy at Inyokern, the population of Ridgecrest has increased considerably.

## Petroglyphs

Petroglyphs—ancient Native American rock art—have been found carved into the desert canyons of the Cosos Mountains, north of Ridgecrest. It is thought that these numerous drawings of men hunting bighorn sheep with spears and arrows could be up to 10,000 years old. In 1964, two of these canyons were declared historical landmarks, and in 1966, Campbell Grant, James W. Baird, and J. Kenneth Pringle began archaeological surveys of these sites. The Navy now allows limited tours into one of these canyons.

## Famous People and Places

Ridgecrest, like many small towns across America, can boast of having raised at least one celebrity. Jennifer O'Dell, the girl who played Veronica on *The Lost World* television show, was born in Ridgecrest on November 27, 1974.

Additionally, twenty miles east of Ridgecrest is the Trona Pinnacles National Landmark. The Trona Pinnacles are tufa spires—some reaching a height of 140 feet—that were formed by underwater algae some 10,000 to 100,000 years ago when Searles Lake formed a link in an interconnected chain of Pleistocene lakes. These 500 calcium carbonate pinnacles rise eerily straight up from the dry lake bed. The formations look as if they belong on a different planet, which may be the reason the area was chosen as a backdrop for the movie *Star Trek V: The Final Frontier*, as well as for the ever-popular movie series, *Planet of the Apes*.

## Ridgecrest Climate

According to quotations collected by Web site owner Pat Jones, Ridgecrest weather is on the "hot" side. As the sayings go, you know you're in Ridgecrest when:

- You can say it is 115 degrees outside without fainting.
- You really *can* fry an egg on the sidewalk.
- You give up dusting daily and just shovel out once a week.
- You learn that a seat belt makes a pretty good branding iron.
- You discover that in July, it takes only two fingers to drive your car.
- Hot water now comes out of both taps.
- The birds have to use pot holders to pull worms out of the ground.
- The potatoes cook underground, and all you have to do to have lunch is to pull one out and add butter, salt, and pepper.
- The trees are whistling for the dogs.
- And, finally, one sad resident once prayed, "I wish it would rain . . . not so much for me, 'cuz I've seen it, but for my seven-year-old."

Holiday on Ice

by Anne C. Watkins

Wintertime in Alabama means bare-limbed trees poking bony, leafless fingers into the sky. Cords of firewood are stacked neatly in preparation for chilly nights, and fragrant wisps of smoke curl up from chimneys. And while the temperatures can be harsh, it's rare to see significant snowfall. It is the accumulation of ice that can be deadly.

One year, just before Christmas, a crippling winter storm devastated our rural section of Alabama. Layers of sparkling, lethal ice coated power lines, telephone poles, and roads. The staccato sounds of cracking branches filled the air, reminiscent of gunfire, as hundreds of trees fractured under the weight. Countless limbs dropped across Alabama's power lines, snapping them like fragile threads and leaving thousands of people without electricity. Businesses were forced to close, and upcoming Christmas celebrations were canceled. Unfortunately, Battleground, our small, close-knit community, wasn't on the road crew's high-priority list when it came to repair and maintenance.

Knowing we'd be without power for quite a while, my husband, Allen, and I were glad that we had kerosene lamps to chase away some of the shadows. Our Christmas tree stood in one corner of the living room, strings of unlit electric lights nestled against the branches. Without the cheerful flashing of the bulbs, the carefully placed ornaments provided the only touch of sparkle and glitz. But even if the electricity had popped back on, the tree and its decorations could never compare to the holiday glory nature had meticulously designed just outside our windows.

I gazed at the landscape, awestruck by the transformation. The fields in front of the house glittered in the moonlight. The scene before me looked like the most beautiful Christmas card that had ever been created. Yet as I looked at our driveway, which had been turned into a shimmering ribbon of ice, I realized that all the main roads were closed and travel would be close to impossible. Glumly, I wondered how in the world we would ever be able to celebrate Christmas with the family.

I sighed with relief when Allen lugged in our old kerosene heater and soon our house was as comfortably warm as it had been before the power outage. We figured out how to cook on top of the heater, and before long we were feasting on coffee, hot soup, scrambled eggs, and odd-looking but tasty biscuits. Things would have been fun, sort of like an indoor camping trip, if we'd only had some clue when the power would be restored.

Christmas Eve arrived clear, starlit, frigidly cold, and still without electricity. My younger brother had invited the family to his house for a holiday supper, and since we lived just a short distance apart, we decided to risk the trek. As Allen skillfully navigated our car down the slippery driveway and along the treacherous road, I stared up at the brilliant diamond points of light in the night sky. Several stars shone brighter than the rest and made me think of the faithful shepherds, all those centuries ago, who had followed a bright star. I gazed in awe at the patterns etched across the sky and was stirred with a sense of connection to those long-ago travelers.

Minutes later, we slid into my brother's yard and then gratefully hustled into the house. To our delight, he had rigged a boat battery to an extension cord, plugged in a lamp, and produced the first electric light we had seen in days. What a delightful, unexpected gift that was!

But I worried about the other members of our family. We had always spent Christmas together, and I knew that the roads the rest of our family would be traveling were perhaps more dangerous than the one we had followed. I prayed they'd make it safely. Soon, they began to straggle in, and we exchanged hugs and shared the special Christmas dinner my sister-in-law had cooked on their gas stove. Finally, we gathered under the lone light bulb to open gifts.

Sitting there, in the midst of my bustling cheerful family, my spirits soared. Our little town may have been dark and days away from restored power, but even that couldn't prevent the light of love from warming my heart. Spending Christmas with my family that evening meant more than anything I could have dreamed of—even electricity.

Lighting of the Tree

by Donna Sundblad

"**I** know it's lookin' kind of puny," the man beside me said, pointing toward the old red cedar that the whole village had gathered around. I'd gotten to know Johns over the last few months when he had joined the sales staff at work. "Hurricane Charley stripped it pretty clean. We lost a good many of the larger trees. We're lucky it's standin'—workin' folk, beachfronters, and social guests have stood shoulder to shoulder for years for the lightin' of this here tree. Look there, you can see the strings of lights clear as day windin' 'round the branches."

The warm Florida sun heated my face as I peered at the tree, spotted the string of light, and nodded. I was happy to have found Johns in the crowd. His stories of life growing up on Gasparilla Island fascinated me.

He nodded to the woman and children who stood beside him. "My family's been here eight generations. This here's my wife, Shelia, and these are our two granddaughters," he explained. Sheila and I exchanged a smile and said hello as one of the children hid behind her and peeked at me.

Johns chuckled. "This one tuggin' on my sleeve is four and her sister there is two." He grinned at his wife. "Shelia, why don't you take them over for a look-see at baby Jesus in the manger?" It only took the little girls a half minute to guide their grandmother across the street toward the manger scene.

Johns nodded toward the manger scene that had been erected beneath the tree and continued our history lesson. "Them statues were donated by the Women's Club," he said. "Each year they added a statue until we had the whole manger scene."

As we waited for the ceremony to begin, Johns explained that he had grown up on the island and that he had made a life on the sea as a fisherman. While he studied the crowd, I studied him. Suddenly his face split into a smile.

"Hey, look over there!" He waved toward the small group gathered north of the tree. A dark-haired man returned the gesture with a smile. "That's Mark and three of his five girls. Good to see a smile on his face. Hurricane Charley peeled the roof right off of his house. They had to move three times while repairs were underway. Does the heart good to see him and his youngsters."

Johns glanced right and left. "By the looks of the crowd, I guess it's almost time to get started," he said. "You know, this ol' tree's been our Christmas tree as far back as I can remember. I can almost hear the washboard band that used to play at the tree lightin' when I was growin' up. Ol' Mary Barnard kept time on that washboard, Louise Futch played the washtub, and Pansy Cost played this thing called a melodica while her sister Billie Jean joined on the piano."

A wry grin played on his lips. "Even movin' that old piano from the Community House was a kindred effort. Everybody chipped in. The men rolled the piano down the street while the women folk scuttled along the sidewalks like a bunch of fiddler crabs, shouting to watch out for this or that." He shook his head, enjoying the memory.

"When I was a teen we started heftin' that heavy Baldwin into the back of a pickup truck. Made it a lot easier. Back then, it didn't matter which church you attended. Movin' the piano, singin' carols to the washboard band, and us kids performin' brought everyone together for the lightin' of the tree."

He pointed toward Fifth Street where it intersected Park Street. "See the police down there blockin' off the street. That yellow crime tape drapin' from one sawhorse to the other just don't look right here. Who would have thought we'd need to block off the street? I remember runnin' barefoot along Fourth Street, not a car in sight. I raced my brother to the tree. We were Boy Scouts, and that year we helped the firemen hang the lights. Back then the fire department was all volunteers. My daddy was one of 'em. All of us boys helped. I was right up there in those branches. Today we've got that fancy new Fire Station, and they use a bucket truck to hang the lights."

He shook his head sadly. "It was more fun climbin' the tree. It's grown since then. In fact, lookin' around, this town's had lots of changes over the years." He reached down to pick up his oldest granddaughter, who had shouldered her way back through the crowd to his side. He jiggled her up and down on his forearm so she could see. "This here bein' a granddaddy is one of them changes!" he said with a grin.

I chuckled along with Johns and talked of my own grand-children. He was a friendly sort, and I enjoyed getting to know him better. Even though I'm a transplanted snowbird, he made me feel as though I belonged.

He leaned over and nudged my arm. "Next year my grand-daughter will be right up there with those kids singin' 'Away in the Manger'. Hear the words? *No crib for a bed.* Makes me think about all the people here in the crowd still out of their homes. Funny how often people visitin' from the North ask us how we can feel the Christmas spirit in the balmy weather. It's not about the temperature." He rested his palm on his chest. "It's what's in here."

A cheer went up in the crowd, and he exclaimed, "Hey, there goes the lights! Hear them cheer? That there's the

Christmas spirit if I ever did hear it." As the crowd moved forward toward the tree, he looked over his shoulder at us one last time. "Have a Merry Christmas! If you come back next year, you'll get to hear my granddaughter sing!"

I, too, found the Christmas spirit around that red cedar. Since then, my mind has often wandered back to Johns and his family and the lighting of the tree on Gasparilla Island. I realized I don't need a sprinkling of snow or a bunch of presents under the tree to bring the Christmas spirit to life for me, either. Like Johns, my family's heritage has instilled that spirit in my heart.

## Silver Magic

by Cheryl K. Pierson

D id you know that there is a proper way to hang tinsel on the Christmas tree?

Growing up in the small town of Seminole, Oklahoma, I was made aware of this from my earliest memories of Christmas. Being the youngest in our family, there was never a shortage of people always wanting to show me the right way to do—well, practically everything! When it came to hanging the metallic strands on the Christmas tree, my mother turned it into a holiday art form.

"The cardboard holder should be barely bent," she said, "forming a kind of *hook* for the tinsel." It was made very clear to me that no more than three strands of the silver magic should be pulled from this *hook* at one time. And, we were cautioned, the strands should be draped over the boughs of the tree gently, to avoid damage to the fragile greenery.

Once the icicles had been carefully added to the already-lit-and-decorated tree, we would complete our "pine princess" with a can of spray snow. Never would we have considered hanging the icicles in blobs, as my mother called them, or tossing them haphazardly to land where they would on the upper, unreachable branches. Hanging them on the higher branches was my father's job, since he was the tallest person I knew—as tall as Superman, for sure. He could do anything—even place the blinking golden star with the blonde angel up on the very highest limb—without a ladder!

Once Christmas was over, I learned that there was also a right way to save the icicles before putting the tree out to the roadside for the garbage man. The cardboard holders were never thrown out. We kept them each year, tucked away with the rest of the re-useable Christmas decorations. Their shiny treasure lay untangled and protected within the corrugated Bekins Moving and Storage boxes that my mother had renamed "CHRISTMAS DECORATIONS" in bold letters with a black magic marker.

At the end of the Christmas season, I would help my sisters undress the tree and get it ready for its lonely curbside vigil. We would remove the glass balls, the plastic bells, and the homemade keepsake decorations we'd made in school. These were all gently placed in small boxes. The icicles came next, a chore we all detested.

We removed the silver tinsel and meticulously hung it back around the little cardboard hook. Those icicles were much heavier than they are now, being made of real metal and not synthetic plastic. They were easier to handle and, if you were careful, didn't snarl or tangle. It was a long, slow process—one that my young, impatient hands and mind dreaded.

For many years, I couldn't understand why everyone—even my friends' parents'—insisted on saving the tinsel from year to year. Then one night, in late December, while Mom and I gazed at the Christmas tree, I learned why.

As she began to tell the story of her first Christmas tree, her eyes looked back through time. She was a child in southeastern Oklahoma, during the Dust Bowl days of the Depression. She and her siblings had gotten the idea that they needed a Christmas tree. They trekked into the nearby woods, cut down an evergreen, and dragged it home. While my grandfather made a wooden stand for it, the rest of the family popped and strung corn for garland. The smaller children made decorations from paper and glue.

"What about a star?" one of the younger boys had asked.

My grandfather thought for a moment. Then he said, "I've got an old battery out there in the shed. I'll cut one from that."

The kids were tickled just to have the tree, but a *star*, too! It was almost too good to be true.

Grandfather went outside. He disappeared around the side of the old tool shed and didn't return for a long time. The children were occupied with stringing the popcorn and making paper chains, but Grandma glanced out the window a few times, wondering what was taking Grandpa so long. The children were so excited that they hardly noticed when he came back inside.

Grandmother turned to him as he shut the door against the wintry blast of air. "What took you so long?" she asked. "I was beginning to get worried."

Grandfather smiled apologetically, and held up the star he'd fashioned. "It took me a while. I wanted it to be just right." He slowly held up his other hand, and Grandmother clapped her hands over her mouth in wonder. Thin strands of silver magic cascaded in a shimmering waterfall from his loosely clenched fist. "It's a kind of a gift, you know, for the kids."

"I found some foil in the battery," he explained. "It just didn't seem right, not to have icicles."

In our modern world of disposable commodities, can any of us imagine being so poor that we would recycle an old battery for the metal and foil, in order to hand-cut a shiny star and tinsel for our children's Christmas tree?

It was only a metal star and some cut-foil tinsel, but for this family it was just the right amount of silver magic, and it was all wrapped up inside a father's love.

# It Isn't Much

by Wendy Stewart-Hamilton

Rainelle, West Virginia, boasts a population of roughly 1,500 people, which is almost a 50 percent increase from what it was when I was a little girl. In the 1970s, the small town's bustling shopping district consisted of two gas stations—one on either side of the town, which was separated by a single stop light—two railroad tracks, a Family Dollar, a Kroger's grocery store, and a Dairy Queen.

The town was small and during Christmastime, decorations were mostly what nature provided: snowy white grounds, red berries on evergreen bushes, red cardinals, green fir trees, and billowing clouds of smoke that puffed up from chimneys on houses scattered across the countryside.

Rainelle was small in size but held a main attraction for me—my grandfather. For the first decade that he was a part of my life, he lived in an even smaller town called Crag, West Virginia. To outsiders like me, the entire area was collectively known as Rainelle. This—my mother's birthplace—was home to more farm animals than residents. It was here, in a small love-filled house, nestled in a holler that was impassable by a car for most of the winter months, I learned the special meaning of Christmas.

My grandfather's simple wooden plank house offered heat—courtesy of West Virginia–mined coal—and boasted light, radiating from a single, bare light bulb in the middle of the room. It was welcoming to me.

My grandfather didn't decorate the house for Christmas as he was of a more conservative generation and was more concerned with necessities than frills. Christmas was about recounting stories of war, the past, the present, and inquiring about his grandchildren's future. Each year, he passed around the Christmas cards received from each of his seven children, a friend or two, and an assortment of great-aunts, uncles, and distantly related cousins. Each one deserved a few minutes of undivided conversation because the sender held an important place in his life, just as I did.

As my family prepared to leave my grandfather's home on Christmas Day, he would go into his bedroom and bring out a bag for my parents containing a warm blanket—each year it was the same, something he knew they could use. And then he would walk into the pantry, pull open a drawer, reach in, and take out two large peppermint sticks for my brother and me. It was a tradition, and each year he said the same thing.

"I know it doesn't seem like much, but I wanted you to know I was thinking of you."

As the years went by, time and commerce caused these large peppermint sticks to shrink, but regardless of their changing size, Grandfather's message did not change. It was the same every year until 1993.

That was the first holiday season I celebrated without my grandfather. Every Christmas since has made me realize how much I crave the simpler days of Rainelle, West Virginia, the old wooden house with outdoor facilities, the impassable roads, and the perfect Christmas present of a single peppermint stick.

It wasn't until many years later that I heard about the comparison between the plan of salvation and the peppermint stick. As the saying goes, the red stripe of the candy represents the blood Jesus shed on Calvary and the white stripe represents a new life we can have and how we can be washed white as snow through God's grace and forgiveness. As I think about that now, I am comforted to know that my grandfather's words have always echoed the words of God: "I know it doesn't seem like much, but I wanted you to know I was thinking of you."

# Home for the Holidays

by Lee Ann Sontheimer Murphy

When I was a young girl, my neighborhood was my heart. All my grandparents lived within walking distance, as did most of my other kin. Their neighbors were also our neighbors, and we knew them well. That idyll ended the year that I turned ten and the packing plant where my father worked closed the day after Thanksgiving.

Although my father went to work on a truck route, our family's financial stability was weakened by his job loss. At the end of the school year, we moved into a mobile home at the other end of the state. The move was necessary for our family. Father was to begin a new career working for the United States Department of Agriculture. But that move took me away from everything familiar.

When I learned we would be going home for Christmas, I became more and more excited as the holidays approached. We'd stay in Granny's two-story frame house—the place that had always been my second home. I would spend days in her company and be able to visit my other grandparents, as well. My cousins and I could play together again! The anticipation was sweet, until my parents informed me that there would be no Christmas tree at Granny's.

I shouldn't have been surprised. Granny had never put up and decorated a Christmas tree once her children were grown. Born in the late 1800s, she had her own way of doing things. Though her husband, who was of German descent, had always made sure their children had a Christmas tree when they were growing up, Granny saw no need to drag a fir into the house and hang baubles on it now that their children were all adults.

I was told not to fuss but to accept the fact that for the first time in my life I would celebrate Christmas without a tree. Some of my bright joy at going home for the holidays dimmed. Though I said nothing, I hoped for a miracle.

Night had already fallen when we pulled up to the familiar house, and I searched the windows for any sign of a tree. There was none. After hugs of greeting and a few kisses, I following Granny up the stairs with a heavy heart. There really would be no tree this year. But when Granny opened the door to my father's old bedroom, I whooped aloud with sudden joy. A scraggly Douglas fir leaned against one wall in the cold room! I turned to my Granny and hugged her with fierce pleasure.

She shook her head quickly. "Don't thank me." Her words sounded stern, but she was smiling. "I had nothing to do with that—thing. Your uncle Roy brought it. He said 'those kids have to have a tree for Christmas.' His doing—not mine."

I slept contentedly that night. I was home for the holidays, and it was all I had hoped it would be. In the morning, we would decorate the Christmas tree. Although it was lopsided and more than a little bare, it was the most beautiful Christmas tree I had ever seen.

by Janet Anderson Hurren
Perry, Utah

Snow was falling. Hard. There was no work to do outside in such inclement weather, and all that was left for my mother to do was think. She was thirty-four when my father died suddenly, following a routine tonsillectomy. We still lived in a two-room house with no running water and dirt floors made hard by her constant sweeping, but she and my father were finally beginning to make a good life together after struggling through the Great Depression. Until that terrible blow, she had been looking toward a future that seemed rosy by comparison. Now, she was a woman alone with no profession and with six children to feed, clothe, and house.

At first, she hadn't a clue how to approach that task, but my mother had sworn to herself and to God that she would do everything in her power to preserve and provide for her family. She thinned, hoed, and topped sugar beets, picked fruit, poached game—anything to put food on the table. The children who were old enough, including me, helped when they could.

My mother made stockings for us from my dad's old socks by sewing a seam, toe to top, to get rid of the holes in the heels and toes. She used the legs of his pants to make bib overalls for us—boys and girls alike. She kept a few chickens and a milk cow, and considered herself fortunate when she scraped together enough money to buy flour for bread. We also needed a garden, so she and my ten-year-old brother plowed the soil with a little push cultivator. Neither was strong enough to push it alone, so my brother pulled it by attaching a rope to it, which formed a harness, and my mother pushed. They took turns pushing and pulling until the task was finished. "A lot like a mule would work," she joked, making do with laughter instead of tears.

Just before the harvest, she and my brother built a root cellar to store the produce that would sustain us during the winter months. When they began, the dirt was compacted and chock-full of little rocks. In order to dig the next day, they carried water in buckets from the spring each evening and soaked the ground, loosening the soil. Working together, our family was doing okay—but just barely.

Time passed, and soon it was time for the holidays. Christmas had never been lavishly celebrated in our household, but we still believed in Santa because he came to our house every year. Every year except this year, though, because my mother had stretched an already thin budget even thinner. She made that clear to us. There was no hidden jar with accumulated change—no chair cushion to shake for the odd nickel or dime. She could stretch her slender resources no further, not even for Christmas.

Besides, she had something else on her mind. Something so awful, really, she cried when she thought no one was looking. She had six children, four girls and two boys. The oldest was thirteen and the youngest was less than a year old. My Dad's childless sister had asked her for one of us. Each one of us breathed an individual sigh of relief when she'd asked incredulously, "Just which one do you think I should give up?"

My aunt had jokingly replied, "I know you can't do it, but I think you're stingy just the same."

What made her cry was that she knew a child given to her sister-in-law could still believe in Santa. There was no poverty at her sister-in-law's house. New clothes, a soft bed, a baby doll—at least one of her children would have them all.

Then—out of the blue—the great idea came to her.

It was simple. All that was required was just a little more work crowded into an already work-filled day. She and my brother would climb up to Perry Canyon and cut Christmas trees to sell. Because they had no boots, they wrapped their feet in burlap chicken-feed sacks in an attempt to keep them warm and dry. After they'd cut the trees, they wrapped them with burlap strips and put one strip over their shoulders to make a harness with which to carry the trees out of the canyon.

They repeated the trip up and back until they were exhausted. Thinking his ten-year-old appeal would sell more trees, my brother offered to stand in front of the small Perry, Utah, grocery store with his small horde until every last one was sold. There wasn't even one left for us. A dollar ninety-eight apiece wasn't much, but Santa would visit our home after all.

Secretly—even I didn't suspect—my mother made one last trip into the canyon on Christmas Eve. When she left the canyon some hours later, she carried out one last tree—a tree that would light up her children's eyes the next morning and welcome the Christ Child into their home.

# Spotlight on Perry, Utah

## Town Facts

**Population:** 2,500
**First incorporated:** 1911
**Original name:** Three Mile Creek.
**Location:** Perry is located in Box Elder County, directly south of Brigham City, eighteen or so miles north of the city of Ogden, along Highway 89. The town is bordered on the east by the Wasatch Mountains and on the west by Bear River Bird Refuge.

## History of Perry

The prime agricultural area, which now constitutes the town of Perry, was first claimed by Orrin Porter Rockwell and his brother, Merrit, in 1851. Due to Indians in the immediate vicinity and the dangers associated with them, the brothers never settled on the land. This was probably just as well as Porter Rockwell was lionized by some, vilified by others, and recognized by all as the Mormon "Destroying Angel."

The area was settled in 1853 by Lorenzo and May Perry, Gustavus Perry, Thomas C. Young Sr., Robert Henderson, and Alexander Perry. At that time, it was called Three Mile Creek. Though Indians continued to crisscross the area at will, they were not hostile as the Rockwells had feared and often bartered wild game for bread. In addition, the Indians graciously taught the white men to cure and tan hides for use in making home-sewn shoes. In May of 1898, the town name was changed to Perry to honor a Latter Day Saint bishop, who had faithfully served his flock for twenty years.

## Industry

Flying J. Inc., begun by the Call family as a small locally owned petroleum company in 1968, operates comfortable truck plazas equipped with showers, telephones, and restaurants. Flying J's have sprouted like mushrooms nationwide and in Canada. Though the corporate offices have been relocated to Ogden, Perryites claim boasting rights because it all started here—Jay Call was one of their own.

Traditionally, Perry has been an agricultural society. Until the last half of the twentieth century, people worked the soil. Fruit orchards, truck and dairy farms, and the like were the primary sources of income. Only after 1958, when Thiokol Chemical Corporation came to Box Elder County, did the citizens diversify and outsiders discover Perry's charms. No sleepy town this. Perry has grown from a few hundred to 2,500 residents. These days, the pink and white lace of flowering fruit trees in the spring have given way to beautiful homes, as the mayor and city council are aggressive in pursuing new business. They have courted and won for the town a Wal-Mart. A multiuse complex, Pointe Perry, west of town is in the planning and early construction phases.

## Transportation

Perry residents helped build the railroad at Promontory Point, which is twenty or so miles west of Perry, but even though tracks pass by the town, trains have never stopped in Perry. The automobile is the primary form of transportation.

## Points of Interest

Bear River Bird Refuge is one of the nation's largest migratory bird refuges, and one of the country's prime wetlands. The section bordering Perry boasts large nesting colonies of various waterfowl, red-winged and yellow-headed blackbirds, and egrets, to name a few.

## Utah's Perfect Peach

It has long been said that if somebody wants to taste the best peaches in the world, they better find Perry, Utah, on the map, and make a pilgrimage there during the month of September. The town center is smack-dab in the middle of Utah's famous Fruitway on Highway 89. From June until October, the stretch from Perry to Brigham City is flooded with people in search of perfect fruits and vegetables. In search of the best peaches known to mankind, one gentleman leaves his home on the island of Hawaii each year to travel to Perry's famous fruit stands. Once there, he hops from Nielson's to Paul's Patch, from Matthew's to Sumida's, and from Tagge's to every little no-name stand in between. "Nothing like them in the world," he says.

## Perry Today

Under the direction of Latter Day Saint Bishop James Nelson, the first meeting cum/schoolhouse in Box Elder County was erected in Perry in 1899. In 1975, the church was converted to a theater, and Sunday services gave way to Monday, Friday, and Saturday theatrical productions. Additionally, the well-maintained, family-owned Walker Cinemas has an eight-movie capacity and provides entertainment for the entire area.

For those wanting to entertain their taste buds, Maddox Ranch House is the place. Established in the early '50s, it has become a destination restaurant known statewide, and as Perry people move on throughout the nation, it is bragged about and never forgotten. Founders Irv and Wilma Maddox and their brainchild have become legendary. One thing is certain—you can't talk about Perry and not talk about Maddox Ranch House.

Over the years, Perry has evolved. Everything has changed, and nothing has changed. The only difference in the town center is that the big red arrow on the west side of the street that formerly pointed to Jesse's Cafe now claims the same fame for Kathy, the present owner, and the Perry School grounds have become the local park and are the focal point for many town functions.

The Police Department is respected, if not feared, by everyone who drives Highway 89. If you're planning a trip to Perry anytime soon, "take heed and don't speed!"

by Marilyn Mosher Shapley

*I* was late for my Latin final. It was a hot Friday afternoon in May, and my exam was scheduled for 5:00 P.M. I had taken my first Latin class fifty years ago when I was a high school freshman. Now, at the age of sixty-two, I was back in school, working toward a college degree.

I opened the back door to the garage and stepped into the hot wet air of South Louisiana. The SUV door handle felt sweaty as I pulled it open. I threw my backpack in and climbed into the driver's seat.

"We've got to hurry, now; no complaining today, Big Guy," I said to my vehicle.

Big Guy was an aging white SUV. I always talked to him. He didn't speak, but he was a good listener. The engine started on the first try, and I backed out of the garage, humming a tune.

"Hear that tune, Big Guy? It's been going around in my head for a couple of weeks now. Why do you suppose I'm humming 'Silver Bells' in this heat?" Big Guy didn't answer, but he did brake nicely when a little red car appeared out of nowhere.

"I remember the first Christmas that song was popular. I was a freshman in high school. Mom and I were hurrying downtown one evening before the holiday to buy my present from Santa—watch out, Big Guy, we've got to go up on the highway."

I maneuvered the car up the access ramp, merged into traffic, and then set the speed control on seventy and settled in for the drive.

"Now, where was I? Oh yes, Christmas of 1952 when I was fourteen. Mom and I were going downtown to buy my present." I let my memory take over as Big Guy followed the familiar route. "My father, who was working two jobs to keep up, came home early that night to watch the little kids so we could go shopping. The latest baby, number six, was a cute round-faced little girl with huge brown eyes, who had been born in April of that year.

"Dad shooed us out the door with a hearty laugh and his big smile." I can see his face so clearly, handsome but tired, the remnants of a bout with Bell's Palsy still evident in the droop of his left eye.

"The door closed behind us, and we were alone in the winter night. Harsh cold air captured our breath and turned it into white vapor and our nostrils stuck together with frost. We hurried down our street past the closed-up neighborhood grocery and crossed a bridge over the creek. Colored pools of neon light spilled onto the snow at the corner gas station—we could see the lights of Main Street ahead, glowing like an enchanted island.

"When we drew closer, we heard 'Silver Bells' pouring out of the loudspeakers on the pine-wrapped light poles. We were both so excited; Mom held my hand tightly, her blue eyes reflecting the lights. She kept her other hand in her pocket to hold the envelope of money that Dad had given her.

"I can still smell wet mittens and winter coats along with perfumes from the cosmetic counter in the big department store. Mom bought me the white wool skirt I wanted so badly." I shook my head with a sigh. "It was so impractical! I spilled ink on it the first time I wore it."

I frowned. *Where had Dad found the money for Mom to buy me anything for Christmas that year?* Mom had only one decent out-of-style dress and Dad's good suit was shiny with wear.

I glanced into the rearview mirror, checked traffic, and then continued with my story. "After the purchase, we stopped at the hat department and tried on hats and struck ridiculous poses." I laughed out loud at the memory. Mother had acted so young and carefree when we were in that store. It was as if I had been shopping with my best friend.

"I can still see our reflection in the mirror," I said wistfully. "Our smiling faces close together."

I chuckled at the mental picture of our shared closeness that I had just painted for Big Guy and wondered briefly if age had caught up with me, carrying on a conversation with an SUV.

"How big-eyed and young we were then, having so much fun that night, both acting like a couple of silly girls with no worries."

I touched the brakes, put my blinker on, and turned onto the exit ramp. As the vehicle gained speed again so did my thoughts. Before long, I had jumped back into the story that Big Guy so anxiously waited to hear.

"When we walked back home, the snow banks were dark and full of shadows. The night was as silent as early morning mass. Our feet made a crunching sound as we walked, and our words hung like crystals in the air."

Big Guy came to a full stop at the red light, and I closed my eyes for a moment.

"Thanks for the present, Mom," I whispered.

Opening my eyes, I looked straight through the intersection. It was as if my mother were standing in front of me, reciting the words today as she had done so many years ago:

"'Remember to be surprised on Christmas morning, so the kids will think Santa brought your present.'"

"I promise," I said.

"Then, like a schoolgirl, Mom shouted, 'Let's run!' She grabbed my hand, and we raced together down the street, our laughter breaking the stillness."

Lost in my memories, I gripped the steering wheel and remembered the feel of her hand in mine. I drove the next few blocks to school in silence. An unexpected cool breeze was blowing when I got out of the vehicle a few minutes later. I was still humming to myself as I climbed the campus hill, but now my mind had returned to the present and was firmly fixed on Latin nouns, gerunds, and participles.

A Special Holiday Mass

by Al Serradell

Even as an eight-year-old, I knew that moving in with relatives—especially at Christmas—was not a good idea. The omens were everywhere that stormy December morning as we left our home in Los Angeles and headed for my aunt Carmen's home in the tiny, wooded hamlet of Monte Rio in northern California. As if the thunderstorm didn't provide enough cause for alarm, our station wagon overheated before we even bid farewell to Orange County.

But my parents refused to cave in.

"We have no choice," my mother explained to me. "Your daddy's been transferred. We have to go where his work takes him." Plus, my mother promised I would like my aunt.

Although I had never met her, Dad used to keep a framed photograph of his sister in the living room. The grainy picture showed a solemn-faced woman standing shoulder-to-shoulder with my father, her right arm wrapped around his waist.

Still unconvinced, I accepted defeat—until the next day when we arrived at Aunt Carmen's. All my doubts returned the moment our car began to climb the steep, muddy road that led to her home. Built beneath a canopy of redwoods, the tall, dark house reminded me of the Haunted Castle on the

Universal movie tour. Snaky vines covered the windows, and the gate swung back and forth on squeaky hinges.

*So this was where I was going to live?*

I expected Boris Karloff to emerge from the front door at any moment. I wasn't disappointed.

From my eight-year-old perspective, my aunt appeared about seven feet tall as she stepped from the house, her bony arms folded like sticks across her chest. Clad in black from the neck to the knees, she had a hawk-like nose and beady eyes that seemed to pierce right through me.

"So this is the boy," she said, her thin lips a colorless slash.

Walking into Aunt Carmen's house, I wondered if she was a vampire. The shades drawn, every room lay shrouded in darkness. Even worse, the place lacked any sign of Christmas, a mere two weeks away.

The next day wasn't much better. While my parents went looking for a suitable home, I had to stay with Aunt Carmen, who spent the entire day cooking and cleaning.

"No television," she snapped. "You'll have to entertain yourself with books."

Her back turned, I decided instead to make a Christmas card. Folding a piece of paper in half, I spent the remainder of the day sketching a picture of Santa riding in his reindeer-drawn sleigh.

I was relieved the following morning when Aunt Carmen left for a doctor's appointment. So while Mom did laundry, I thought up a new game to play—pretending I was on a pilgrimage to the Vatican to see the Pope. Only I needed props. First, I removed a statue of the Holy Family from the dining room hutch, carefully placing Mary, Joseph, and Baby Jesus in my little red wagon. I figured they would give me leverage when I asked His Holiness to intervene for me by asking God to let my family go back home for Christmas.

The ceremony, held inside my aunt's storage shed, was simple. I started with The Lord's Prayer, tossed in a few Hail Mary's, and then made my request. "Please," I added. "I'll never beg for another thing again."

The ritual complete, I started to leave. That's when the accident happened. I must've turned the wheels too sharply, for the wagon tipped over and out tumbled the Holy Family. Thankfully, they landed on a pile of magazines or they would've busted into a kajillion pieces. As I returned them to the wagon, however, I saw that the baby Jesus' nose was missing, obviously broken off in the tumble. I checked the floor around the wagon but couldn't find the severed nose.

Panic-stricken, I decided to return the statue to the house ASAP, hoping that no one, especially my dad's ever-lurking sister, would notice that Jesus was now disfigured.

A few days passed in miserable anticipation. Then, one afternoon, the dreaded confrontation arrived.

"You," my aunt said, pointing a bony finger at me. "Explain something to me."

My heart sank. No doubt she'd found the statue.

She jerked a piece of paper from her apron pocket. "This."

I looked down at the object in question. It was the Christmas card I'd made. I couldn't believe I'd forgotten it on the kitchen table.

"Read it to me," she said.

Clearing my throat, I obeyed: "Thank you, Aunt Carmen, for making this our new home. May all your Christmas wishes come true. Love, Alberto."

I'd barely gotten the last line out when she threw her arms around me tightly.

"My son! I am so proud of you."

I couldn't believe my ears. Then, startling me further, she kissed the top of my head. I could've sworn she had tears in her eyes. "That is the sweetest Christmas card I ever received. The first one that was ever made with love."

So the ceremony in the shed had worked! God had granted me a miracle. Not the one I expected, but a miracle, nonetheless. In that instant, my feelings toward the old woman also changed. She never looked at me with cruel, beady eyes again.

Over the years, I have often thought of that Holy Family statue and Aunt Carmen's hard facade.

"She never married, you know," Dad told me after her funeral years later. "Her fiancée died a month before their wedding day. I guess she just went into mourning and didn't come out of it."

I never did find the Holy Family statues after that. According to rumors, it had been sold in an estate sale when Aunt Carmen went into a nursing home, a few months before her death. But I've always hoped that whoever owned it would treasure it as I still do—and that someday they would get the baby Jesus' nose fixed.

## One Bright Night

by Helen Luecke

"**C**ome on, Babs," I yelled to my older sister. "It's time to go!"

I pulled my green cap down over my ears and slipped on my matching mittens. Tonight was a special time for Babs and me. We were going to sing Christmas carols for some of our neighbors.

I buttoned my coat and skipped across the room to the calendar. "Look, Momma, December 23, 1946—just two more days until Christmas!"

She smiled and wrapped a woolen scarf around my neck. "Cozy, you stay close to Babs and sing real pretty. When ya'll get back, Daddy and I will be waiting with hot chocolate and cookies."

Just then Babs walked into the kitchen, pulled on her red cap and gloves, and headed out the back door. I followed her out into the cool crisp night where a million stars sparkled in the sky.

Babs turned around and looked at me. "Do you remember the four songs I taught you?"

"I think so," I answered.

Our first stop was at the Murdock house. A Christmas tree decorated with bright colored lights and shiny reflectors stood in the window.

Babs straightened my cap and whispered, "'Silent Night' is our first song."

As soon as we began to sing, Mrs. Murdock opened the door. I made it through the whole song without making any mistakes.

"That was beautiful," Mrs. Murdock said, smoothing down her apron. "You deserve an apple." She handed one to each of us. "You tell your family Merry Christmas."

I put the apple in my pocket, thanked Mrs. Murdock, and followed Babs to the next house on our list. The gravel crunched beneath our feet as we walked up the driveway to Miss Hammond's house.

"I'll be glad when I'm old enough to be in Miss Hammond's class at school," I said wistfully as I moved closer to Babs. "What song now?"

"'Hark The Herald Angels Sing'."

Miss Hammond turned on the porch light and watched us sing. I hummed most of the song.

"Thanks for singing for me," Miss Hammond said. She held out two yellow pencils with tiny red bows tied around the top. "Babs, you sing real well," she said as Babs accepted the present. "And Cozy, you sure can hum."

Walking across the street to the Newman house, I had a great idea. "Let's sing, 'Jingle Bells' because I know every bit of it," I said excitedly.

Babs stopped and looked at me in surprise. "No! We're singing true Christmas songs. Don't you know what Christmas is all about?"

"Yes," I shot back. "Santa Claus and presents."

Babs let out a sigh. "Cozy, you have it all wrong. Look at those stars. See how bright they are? Well a long, long time ago a bright star was seen all over the world. That star announced the birth of Jesus." She moved closer to me. "Haven't you been listening to your Sunday School teacher?"

"Yes," I muttered.

Babs continued as though she hadn't heard me. "That star led the three Wise Men to Jesus," she said as we hurried up the five steps of the Newman's porch.

"It's 'Joy To The World' this time," Babs whispered.

I nodded, pleased. I knew all the words to that song.

"My, my," Mrs. Newman said when we were finished. "That sure was pretty." Humming another verse, she handed us a candy cane. "How's the first grade, Cozy?"

"Just fine," I answered.

"What grade are you in, Babs? The fourth?"

"Yes, ma'am," Babs answered.

Mrs. Newman stood with her hands on her round hips. "You girls come over, after Christmas. I'll be getting my new Avon inventory, and I'll go through my old stuff. There's lots of perfume and lipstick samples ya'll can have."

"Thanks," we answered.

Giggling, we ran down the steps.

"I hope there are some perfume samples of To a Wild Rose, I confided. "I just love that smell, and the bottle is so cute."

Babs shook her head in the way of older sisters. Then she took my hand and pulled me along. "When we get home, you can sing 'Jingle Bells' for Momma and Daddy."

"All by myself?" I questioned.

Babs nodded and continued to explain the true meaning of Christmas to me as we walked to the Lester house. "The three Wise Men brought presents of gold, frankincense, and myrrh for the baby Jesus."

"What's frankincense and myrrh?" I asked.

"They were kind of like spicy candles and sweet perfume. But they were really expensive."

I tried to think of a candle or perfume that cost a lot. All I could think of were birthday candles and To a Wild Rose perfume.

Mr. Lester requested all three verses of 'It Came Upon A Midnight Clear'. I wasn't thinking about caroling anymore as much as I was thinking about perfume and birthdays, but I still managed to hum the last two verses.

"Here," Mr. Lester said. "You each get a nickel."

"Thanks," we yelled in unison as we hurried down the steps.

As we started home, Babs's voice turned serious. "There's one thing I don't understand. Christmas is Jesus' birthday and the Wise Men brought him presents." She turned to me with a frown on her face. "Right?"

"Right," I answered.

A light snow had begun to fall silently all around us, muting the sound of our steps and making it seem like the sound of her voice and our breathing was the only thing that existed. "Don't get me wrong, Cozy," she explained. "I like getting presents. But it seems like we're giving to the wrong person."

I thought about it for a moment. Babs was right. I pursed my lips and nodded. "Let's put our nickel in the offering plate Sunday," I suggested.

Babs smiled and grabbed my hand. Together, we ran toward the soft yellow glow of the welcoming lights of home. The moment we stepped inside the door, Momma helped us out of our coats and caps. She smiled proudly.

"Did everyone like your singing?"

"Yes, and they all gave us a present." Babs said.

"I love our neighbors," I added. "They're just like family."

As the fragrance of cookies and hot chocolate danced all around us, Daddy joined the conversation. "Now, you two sing for us."

Without hesitation, Babs and I walked to the center of the room and stopped in front of the Christmas tree. As I turned and gazed at the faces of my family, I felt love fill the room. It was as if something inside of me blossomed like a flower opening up under the bright yellow sun.

Before Babs could say anything, I spoke up, loud and clear. "We're going to sing a song for you that tells the real meaning of Christmas. It's not about Santa Claus." I glanced at my sister. "Or jingle bells, or presents." Babs squeezed my hand gently, her face reflecting exactly what I was feeling at that moment. And as I began singing the first verse to 'Away in a Manger', I heard my sister's voice join in. I am not sure there has been anything in my life since that was quite as symbolically perfect as that moment.

Shared Memories

by Terri Meehan

$\mathcal{I}$ love a good story—especially one about holiday memories that make you feel all warm and cozy inside. One of my favorites is the story of an especially memorable Christmas Eve in 1945 when my dad was thirteen years old.

Dad's family moved from Morrisdale, Pennsylvania, to Osceola Mills in 1940 when my grandfather found work in the mining industry. Osceola Mills was a typical small town where everyone knew everyone else, and the family loved their new home.

It was gray and cold with a sprinkling of snow flurries in the air the day my father moved into the neighborhood, but the weather did little to dampen his mood. He was excited with his new surroundings—especially the large empty field next door to his house, complete with a pond. He looked at his older sister, Kate, and smiled. "Just think of the fun we'll have this winter once the pond freezes!"

She frowned. "What's it to you? You don't even own a pair of skates."

It was true. Dad didn't even know how to skate. It was difficult times. It was tough making enough cash for necessities such as food and paying the monthly bills. Dad was the middle child with eight other brothers and sisters and knew the chance of his getting skates was not good, but with dogged determination, he refused to give up on his dream.

Soon after moving into town, Dad and his brother Bill become delivery boys for the local paper, which helped with family finances. Since it was only three weeks before Christmas, any extra income would be needed to buy presents. Grandfather was doing what he could by accepting overtime work in the mines. He left before dawn and didn't return until late in the evening. He would walk in the door exhausted and covered with black coal dust.

In an attempt to keep the dust trail out of her house, each night as Grandmother heard him approach the front door, her voice would ring out from the kitchen, "Be sure you shake out your pant legs on the steps before you come indoors!"

Working in a coal mine was dirty work, and women's voices—shouting much the same as my grandmother shouted—could be heard in all the houses along the lane where hard-working men were returning home from the mines. It was hard times everywhere, but togetherness kept the families strong.

Though my grandfather used a pickup truck for work, he was also able to purchase a 1939 secondhand car for family needs. Trouble was, it seldom started on the first try. More times than not, he roused the neighbors each Saturday morning when he tried to get it started so my grandmother could go into town and purchase the weekly groceries. The engine was as loud as fireworks exploding on the Fourth of July. To add to the problems, my grandfather could only afford one set of license plates. To rectify this, he put the set of plates onto whichever vehicle he was driving on that particular day.

Grandfather received a small Christmas bonus, so on Christmas Eve he planned to go into town to purchase gifts for his family. As he tells the story, he was humming 'O Holy Night' to himself as he performed his license-swapping act in his driveway when a policeman happened to be driving by. My dad and his brother had just finished delivering papers when they watched in shock as their father was hauled away in the police car. They ran into the house, screaming at the top of their lungs.

My grandmother ran down the stairs to find out what the commotion was about. As soon as she burst into the room, they shouted: "The cops took Daddy away!"

Wringing her hands fitfully, my grandmother asked the neighbors if they would drive her to the police station. They agreed, and within minutes Grandmother was pleading for Grandfather's release. But no matter what she said, the arresting officer refused. A crime had been committed.

"It's against the law to change license plates," the office explained. "He needs to buy another set of license plates."

My grandfather's heart fell. He knew he couldn't afford another set of license plates. It was beginning to look as though he'd have to spend the holiday behind bars. Just then, Mrs. Crane, one of the clerks, walked into the courthouse and recognized my grandfather.

She looked at the officer. "What's this?" She asked. "You can't lock up this man. He has nine children and a wife to support!"

Her outburst shed a different light on the incident, and the officer relented. Relief shone in my grandfather's eyes. In fact, Dad has hinted that Grandfather would have kissed the woman had it not been for the fact that Grandmother was there watching.

As Grandfather watched his children open their Christmas presents the next morning, he knew it wasn't the material gifts they found in their stockings that put the smiles on their faces. The entire family was thrilled just to be together again.

Later that morning, as my father and his siblings enjoyed their new gifts from Santa, there was a knock on the door. When Grandmother opened it, she was surprised to see the policeman who had arrested my grandfather. He smiled and presented my grandfather with a check to pay for another set of license plates for the car.

"I am sorry, I didn't realize you had so many children to support," he explained sheepishly. "I want to help out—Merry Christmas!"

The family was surprised a few minutes later when Mrs. Crane also paid them a visit. "Please take this food for your Christmas dinner," she said, offering my grandmother a large parcel. "And let me know if there's anything else you need."

The kindness and generosity of these two individuals brought tears to my dad's eyes. He didn't receive the ice skates that he'd been wishing for, but he hardly noticed.

"What I received that Christmas is the best gift of all. It can never be lost or stolen. It remains forever in my heart," he said.

As I travel thousands of miles each year to return home, my father's words reflect exactly what I'm thinking. Sharing memories is the best Christmas gift.

The Gift of a Smile

by Shirley P. Gumert

t the end of each Christmas parade held in Kilgore, Texas, in the late 1930s, Santa Claus rode into town on a fire truck. The real highlight followed when the mayor flipped a switch to turn on hundreds of red and blue electric lights that crisscrossed above the downtown streets. At the same time, the words "Merry Christmas" and "Happy New Year," which hung suspended between several nearby oil derricks were suddenly illuminated. But the brightest and best of all came last. Clutching my mother's hand, I stood in awe as all over town big, beautiful electric stars atop the dozens of oil derricks flashed on.

On parade night, the downtown area was filled with people and joyous sounds. Stores stayed open later, and everyone stopped to visit and check out the merchants' wares. One such Christmas, I recall how my mother lifted me up to see a jeweler's display—a miniature snow village with tiny, moving figures—as well as other store windows, which were decorated with paintings by high school students.

When we reached Wacker's dime store, I pulled my mother inside. I liked to peek over the counters, lined with glass dividers, and gaze at the toys: metal cars, airplanes, marbles, Tinker Toys, Lincoln Logs and dolls. I wanted to see everything and

Mother seldom shopped. She had learned, during the Depression years, how to *make do*. Today, she would have probably become a designer of children's clothing. Back then, she was just another mother using scraps and remnants to make her childrens' clothing. Now, she could become a noted doll maker. Then, she was just using materials at hand to make soft dolls and doll clothes. Sewing was both necessity and joy to her.

I already knew she was making me Raggedy Ann and Andy dolls. She had been unable to keep the project a secret. Together we had read the Johnny Gruelle books and decided on the right colors.

I knew that after spending hours making them, Mother would wrap them in great, lumpy packages to go under our pine Christmas tree. They'd be no surprise come Christmas morning, but I also knew the dolls were to be my biggest Christmas gift. Even though I knew about those dolls, when I peered over the counter at Wacker's that day and saw an eight-inch-tall brown-haired doll, dressed in a glued-on costume, I was transfixed. At first sight, that fifty-cent doll was *my* doll.

I looked up at my mother. "I really want that doll," I said. Mother picked the doll up, looked it over, and then set it back down.

"How much money do you have?" she asked.

"A dime," I answered.

"It costs fifty cents. That's high, for a doll."

But I couldn't take my eyes off of the beautiful doll. "Look," I pleaded. "Look at her. Look at her smile at me. Isn't she beautiful?" I sighed wistfully. "She's the only doll I want."

"But you don't have fifty cents. Maybe later . . . "

"What if someone else buys her?"

Mother shook her head. "Not likely. But I guess you can put the doll on layaway, if you think you can pay it out, yourself."

Wacker's was probably the only store where a merchant would let a young girl buy a fifty-cent doll on layaway as long as she promised to pay ten cents a week. I laid down my dime and reached forward to touch the doll moments before she was tagged for layaway.

When I got home, I went to my room and rattled my piggybank, counted pennies, and thought of ways to earn money. A few days later, I saved the nickel my dad gave me for a Hershey's bar. Sometime later, a dime appeared in my piggybank, mysteriously, accompanied by my uncle Tommy's laugh. I ran an errand for my grandmother, and she gave me a nickel. And—wonder of wonders—while I was watching trains at the Kilgore depot, I saw my favorite engineer (I called him "My Man") come through, blowing the whistle on his steam locomotive. As he waved, he tossed me a coin I seldom saw . . . a quarter! I could get my doll out of layaway, in time for Christmas!

Meanwhile, my mother continued to work on Raggedy Ann and Andy. She consulted me about yarn for their hair and what to use as Raggedy Andy's magical wishing stick. "Here," she said, as she handed a pencil to me, "You mark their smiles." When I looked at her in surprise, she smiled encouragingly. "You do it. You mark their smiles, and I'll sew them on. That way they'll always smile right at you."

I took the pencil and carefully marked their smiles and watched as Mother embroidered them on. Sure enough, when she was finished, she wrapped the two dolls and put them underneath our Christmas tree. That same afternoon, she walked with me to Wacker's to get the other doll I'd chosen and paid for. I was so thrilled that I skipped all the way home.

On Christmas night, I sat outside on our porch steps with my three new dolls. Together, we looked up at the shining stars on oil derrick tops and let the wonder of Christmas seep in.

Many years later, when my mother and I were going through fabric scraps, I asked if she would make another set of Raggedy Ann and Andy dolls for my two-year-old daughter.

"Mine are too special for anyone else to play with," I explained.

"Do you still have them?" She asked.

"Of course," I replied in surprise. "I always will. I need to see them smile, right at me," I said, remembering her words of long ago.

Mother turned away quickly and began gathering fabrics, but not before I saw the small smile on her face. It wasn't until then that I realized she hadn't known that the dolls she had made for me had always meant more to me than the store-bought doll. As I watched the emotion flit across her face, my heart skipped a beat, and I made another discovery. Perhaps, until that moment, even I had not known how very precious those dolls were to me.

Handfuls of Pennies

by Ella Birdie Jamison, as told to Norma Favor
Beetown, Wisconsin

**E**lla was disillusioned.

This year, even the lighted candles shining from the evergreen-trimmed windows, the sound of sleigh bells, and the laughter of children sledding on the snow-covered hills had failed to bring Ella the usual Christmas expectation.

It was Christmas Eve in the little town of Beetown, Wisconsin. Her twin brother, Buzz, was sledding in the moonlight with his boisterous friends. Mother was tending the telephone switchboard located on their kitchen wall, and right now Ella had no idea where her father was or what he was doing. Earlier, she had helped him wait on customers in their little store below their apartment. When the last customer had left the building, Papa had locked the store door and sent Ella upstairs. Now, she gazed out of the window of the upstairs parlor at the snow-covered town below and hoped Papa would come upstairs and grab her in his usual bear hug and laugh her out of her melancholy.

Ella glanced at the wrapped presents underneath the Christmas tree and sighed. Weeks ago, she had helped Papa unpack the Christmas merchandise and place the toys, books, and games on the store shelves. She had looked at and touched every potential present, and she knew some of it was under the tree with her name tagged on it. She wished that just once she would be surprised with a wonderful gift that she had never laid eyes on. When she had shared her thoughts with Papa tonight, he had just looked at her with twinkling eyes and smiled. Just thinking of his amusement at her misery made her so mad that she stamped her high-button shoes and flounced to the horsehair sofa, her long black braid switching angrily.

As she sat pouting, she heard noises coming from the store below. Cautiously, she crept down the stairway and opened the door a crack. In the near dark, she saw someone at the till. The sound of clinking coins fell softly in the silent store. Ella gasped in dismay as the large dark shape turned. It was Papa! *Why was Papa stealing from the till?* And why was he dressed so strange? Amazement and a trickle of fear flushed her chubby cheeks.

Papa paused for a moment as if considering something and then beckoned her over to him. Silently, he handed her a handful of small brown-paper bags. He showed her how to put a handful of pennies into each of the bags while he put on a red velvet jacket trimmed with white fur and a red, tasseled, velvet hat. Ella exclaimed that he looked just like Santa Claus. Papa only winked and told her to run and put on her warmest hat, coat, and her muff. He was going somewhere, and she was coming with him. In a wink, Ella was back. Before she could take another breath, Papa had her snuggled in their sleigh amid boxes filled with turkey-dinner fixings. The box of penny-filled paper bags sat between them.

With a toss of his mane, their horse trotted away, pulling the sleigh quietly through the snow. No one saw them slip down the short, snow-covered main street and out onto the country road. Ella was speechless. It was all so magical.

As they approached a shabby little shack, she heard the laughter and cries of little children. Papa put his finger to his lips and gave her a little bag of pennies to carry. He hoisted a large box of groceries, and they sidled up to the sagging porch. Papa put the box close to the door and motioned Ella to run back to the sleigh. Papa slowly and quietly opened the front door of the house and tossed the bag of pennies as far into the room as he could and then raced to the sleigh and whipped the horse into a fast trot. As they flew away, she heard delighted screams of joy. Papa beamed at the sound, and Ella felt the stirring of something magical.

For the next few hours, they sped from house to house.

After the sleigh was empty, they headed back to the store. Papa strode in, lit as many lamps as he could, and opened up the store for business. A few children were already waiting on the porch, shivering in their thin coats. Each child clutched a small paper bag of pennies.

Ella's heart gave a lurch when she noticed that Papa had lowered all the prices on the toys and candy. She looked at the children, and her smile knew no bounds. She had never heard such a wonderful commotion as those children made as they spent their pennies. Nor had she ever seen such happiness. Her heart was filled with joy and pride. She looked at each child in turn, and then she raised her gaze to her father's beaming face. That Christmas, Papa had given her the best gift of all. He had shared with her the gift of giving.

# Spotlight on Beetown, Wisconsin

---

## Town Facts

**Population:** 90

**Location:** Beetown is situated in Beetown Township, between the towns of Lancaster, Cassville, and Blooming-ton, Wisconsin. Beetown lies in a holler, protected by the hills of Grant County.

---

## African-American Pioneers Settle Area

In 1848, Charles and Caroline Shepard, and their three children—Harriet, John, and Mary—and Charles's brother Isaac, started one of the first African-American pioneer settlements in the state of Wisconsin. The community sat on the outskirts of Beetown and was called Pleasant Ridge. The Shepards were freed slaves of William Horner. When the Horner family packed up and moved to Wisconsin in the search for better farmland, the Shepards followed suit. Pleasant Ridge was home to freed slaves, fugitive slaves, and European immigrants. One of the state's first integrated schools was erected in Pleasant Ridge, and today the Pleasant Ridge Cemetery marks the spot where this historical farming settlement once stood. Recently, Old World Wisconsin, a living history museum, has recreated the nineteenth-century community, complete with school, church, community hall, and a replica of the Pleasant Ridge Cemetery.

## Naming of a Town

In 1927 a windstorm swept through the area, uprooting a big tree. In the process, the storm uncovered a new work for locals—iron ore mining. Stuck in the roots of the downed tree was a big nugget of lead ore. Of course, the townsfolk all wanted a closer look, but in addition to hiding lead ore beneath it, the tree housed an unusually large number of bees within its branches, and they weren't letting anyone near their home—downed or not! The news about the "bee town" spread far and wide, and before long residents adopted the name.

Eventually the bees were disposed of and area miners as well as miners from Galena, Illinois, began mining in earnest. The Atkinson mine, which had been abandoned for some time, recently was closed to the public to prevent accidents. Though lead mining ended many years ago, John Jamison—the third generation to own and operate Beetown's famous general store—recalls colleting lead from the creek that runs behind the store, with his three sisters when they were children.

## The General Store

The Jamison Store, founded in 1897, is still in existence today and is still family owned and operated. John saw a need, and like any good businessman, took advantage of the opportunity and built a store with an upstairs apartment. Little did he know that his son, Paul, and his grandson, John Paul, would live in the upstairs apartment and own and operate the same store that he had brainstormed so many years before. Neither could he know that it would still be a prospering business in the twenty-first century.

John Paul Jamison has been working in the store since 1958 and has recently placed the store on the market. John says he hopes to find a buyer who is willing to keep the store open. "Beetown folks rely on the store for more things than just groceries," he explained. "Folks call down here for information, for historical facts—sometimes they just call to see what day it is!" More importantly, if the Jamison Store closed, Beetown residents would be forced to travel upward of ten miles each time they needed supplies.

## Six-Year-Old Cheddar Cheese

Schurman's Wisconsin Cheese Country Inc. has been part of Wisconsin's rich tradition of cheese making for over seventy years, and Beetown residents are proud to call it their own. For the past twenty-five years, Schurman's has provided custom cheese packaging and private labeling for wholesalers and distributors across the country. Additionally, Schurman's operates a cheese outlet store and proudly displays more than thirty varieties of cheese. Among the cheeses is Beetown's famous Cheddar cheese, which has been aged for six long years.

## Beetown Trivia

In 1897, the first John Jamison was so intrigued with the invention of the telephone that he rode a bicycle to Chicago three times to figure it all out. Once he had it all down pat, he started Beetown's first phone cooperative, Farmers' Telephone Company, from his home above the Jamison Store. The first phones were placed in Dr. Blackbourn's house and in the blacksmith's shop. Farmers' Telephone Co. recently was sold to Television Data System (TDS) Telecom.

Rollo Jamison, nephew of John Adam Jamison, was born in Beetown in 1899. Rollo was one of those individuals who is destined for big things—in this case, it was his antiques and artifact collection. Even when he was a child, Rollo was collecting arrowheads on the family farm. At final count, his collection numbered somewhere around 20,000 items. Currently, the collection is on display at the Rollo Museum in Platteville, Wisconsin.

At 1:30 in the afternoon on October 28, 1849, an unexpected phenomenon occurred in Beetown. According to eyewitnesses, the sky darkened—reminiscent of an eclipse—terrifying the residents and going down in the record books as Beetown's "dark day."

Several tragedies struck Beetown in its early days. The first was an 1850 cholera epidemic. In one week's time, more than forty-two residents succumbed to the disease, and the town was nearly turned into a ghost town. The second tragedy came in the form of a flood in early 1851 when heavy rains fell, raising the river to a "height before unknown." In the middle of the night, clad only in their nightclothes, Beetown residents scrambled from their homes just inches ahead of the rising waters.

Christmas Caroling

by Jewell Johnson

The five of us trudged down the path, our overshoes crunching on the snowpacked road. At the corner, we stopped under a streetlight.

"Where should we go now?" Bobby asked.

"How about Mr. Blake's?" Marilyn answered.

Our eyes peered into the darkness to see the outline of the Blake mansion, looming on the hill a half mile from where we stood. We had sung Christmas carols for Widow Sorvik, the Bengstons, Ben Nelson, and other nearby families. It had never occurred to us to venture beyond our neighborhood and certainly not to sing for the proprietor of Blake's Dry Goods Store.

It wasn't that kids in our northern Minnesota town didn't have plenty to do. We could have been ice-skating—now that some kind person had hung a light bulb over the pond—or, since it was Monday night, we could have been home listening to Lux Radio Theatre. We also could have been reading Lincoln's Emancipation Proclamation for history class, but that was low on our list. No, it wasn't boredom that sent us caroling on this subzero night a week before Christmas. We liked singing carols, and we knew all the songs by heart. For weeks we'd been practicing "Silent Night," "Joy to the World," and others for church and school.

Yet, it was more than that. It was the magic of the season, the desire to share the joy of Christmas.

"It's pretty far up there," I said, studying the winding lane to the mansion.

"Yeah, and Mr. Blake's hard of hearing," Earl added.

"Besides, he never goes to church," Bobby said. "He doesn't even like Christmas carols."

We had overheard our parents speculate on the reasons Mr. Blake didn't darken the church door. Some said it was because he was too deaf to hear the preacher. Others thought the town's only millionaire was excused from ordinary things like church-going.

"If we sing for him, maybe he'll give us a candy bar!" Mary Ann exclaimed, her high-pitched voice piercing the evening air. She clapped her red mittens together, pleased to have come up with the idea.

Mary Ann's comment clinched the deal for us. Every child within twenty-five miles knew Mr. Blake often handed out free chocolate bars to children in his store on Saturdays. So that night, the five of us went on a mission.

The Blake mansion stood set apart from the rest of the town, situated on a five-acre tract, surrounded by giant cottonwoods, elms, and maple trees. The bare branches of these trees creaked and swayed above us eerily as we trudged up the snowpacked lane. When we got closer, we realized only a couple of lights glowed in the huge house.

"Do you think he'll hear us?" Bobby asked, raising his eyes to the window above us.

"No, but Mrs. Rustad, his housekeeper, will," I said.

We stood knee-deep in snow and sang the first line to "O Little Town of Bethlehem," our voices rising and falling to the melody. But when we were finished with the song, no one had appeared.

"Let's try 'Joy to the World'," Bobby said, stomping his feet to keep warm. "We can get loud on that."

We strained our voices, all the while craning our necks for a glimpse of Mr. Blake at the window. When no face appeared a second time, I sighed in frustration.

"He can't hear us." I said.

Reluctantly, we turned to find our way back to the road. But before we had taken no more than a couple of steps, the front door opened, and Mrs. Rustad appeared in the shadows, hugging a pink sweater around her checkered housedress.

"Children!" She said anxiously. "Would you like to come in and sing for Mr. Blake?"

"Yes!" we shouted.

Hopping over the snowdrifts like arctic kangaroos, we pushed our way toward the back entrance of the mansion, and followed Mrs. Rustad to a small, unheated room.

"Wait here," she said, then exited the room, leaving us to gaze in awe at our surroundings. Within minutes, the door swung open again, and Mr. Blake stepped into the room.

"You came to sing for me?" he asked. His stern gray eyes swept over the five of us as he waited for his answer. We nodded solemnly. His gaze traveled across our faces, then he stabbed a finger at Bobby. "What are your names?"

"Bobby Carlson," said Bobby. Turning to his side, he pointed to Mary Ann. "This is my little sister. She's six."

"Speak louder, children," Mrs. Rustad said. "Mr. Blake is hard of hearing."

"Earl's my name," Earl shouted. "And this is Marilyn and Jewell."

Then, without any further ado, Mr. Blake adjusted his hearing aid, cupped his right hand over his ear, and fixed his eyes on the linoleum. It was time to sing.

*"Joy to the world! The Lord is come,"* we sang with all our might. Then, softer, we sang "Silent Night" and "O Little Town of Bethlehem."

As the music faded, Mrs. Rustad wiped her eyes. Mr. Blake cleared his throat and shifted his feet, but his eyes did not meet our gaze. What followed was an awkward moment when no one moved, and no one spoke.

Finally Bobby said, "Well, we'll be going." Four of us shuffled toward the door. Only Mary Ann stood and stared at Mr. Blake, her blue eyes as round as marbles.

Suddenly, Mr. Blake shouted, "Wait!" He left the room and returned, holding a brown box. *Ah! Candy bars!* We thought, collectively.

Mary Ann smiled as she selected the first chocolate bar. "Thank you!" She shouted loud enough for Mr. Blake to hear. Once we were outside, we took off our mittens and unwrapped the candy.

"Wasn't that nice of him?" Mary Ann's shrill voice echoed in the stillness. "I sure like Mr. Blake."

"Let's sing!" Bobby yelled, his enthusiasm reflecting what we all felt.

As the sound of our voices filled the night air, it blocked the sound of snow crunching at our feet and tree boughs rubbing against one another eerily. The beautiful words echoed through the dark streets and alleys, loud and clear, and behind us, it resounded in the heart of the town's one millionaire, who stood at the window and watched us walk away.

Before Portland

by Patti Mattison Livingston

The boy next door had a toy dump truck. It really dumped, and I really wanted it. That boy wouldn't even let me touch it. Daddy was a civil engineer, bossing construction crews; he often took me to watch his men driving steam shovels and trucks. I knew more about dump trucks than that boy!

I was in first grade, learning to read and write, so I asked Daddy to help me write a letter to Santa Claus, asking for my own dump truck. The year was 1929. I know because I liked to lie on the floor sounding out words in the newspaper, and when I came upon those puzzling numbers, I asked my mother—I called her Mudgie—what they meant. She explained that years have numbers and 1929 was that year's number. My kingdom, where I reigned as an only child, hadn't yet suffered from the historic 1929 stock market crash.

Mudgie, Daddy, and I lived in Roseburg, Oregon, for now. Our real home, where the rest of the family lived, was Medford, another small town in Oregon. But Daddy worked for a power company and that kept the three of us on the move.

For Christmas, we were going back to Medford, to Mama's House. Mama—my version of Grandmamma, which was the name she preferred, and Grampa Ahbo, which was the best I could do with the name Grandfather Albert—were my mother's parents. They lived on a pear orchard at the edge of Medford. Mudgie's younger brother, George, lived with them. Georgie treated me with affectionate scorn, but sometimes gave me rides in his Studebaker coupe, which made him tolerable.

Daddy's parents, Grandmother and Grandfather, also lived in Medford. Before we moved to Roseburg, Grandfather and Grandmother had gone to Portland for a long time. The tight-faced family whispered scary words like *cancer* and *opera-tion,* and when they returned home, Grandfather stayed in his pajamas all the time, looking very white. He didn't build furniture anymore, not even doll furniture for me.

It was raining when we started over the mountain on Christmas Eve day, and I was worried that Santa Claus wouldn't be able to find me at Mama's House. I wondered, too, if Grandfather would still be wearing pajamas all day.

Mama's House smelled of ginger, cinnamon, and Christmas tree. Mama hugged me close and handed me some cranberry garlands to hang on the tree, and then after supper Grampa Ahbo read me *The Night Before Christmas*. I tried to read with him, but he was reciting from memory and not following the pages, so I just listened and looked at the pictures.

That night, when I went to bed on a cot in Grampa Ahbo's study, I couldn't sleep. Once, after the lights were all out, I heard rustling in the front room and peeked. Mudgie was putting a bulging cotton stocking under the tree. That didn't surprise me. I had poked around in our closets at home and discovered the stuffed stocking. I knew she helped Santa with that part of Christmas, but would Santa know I was at Mama's House?

The next morning, I roused the family before dawn. While Grampa Ahbo built up the fire in the big wood stove, I poured the stocking's treasures out: toys and candy and some gor-geous marbles. Then I searched among the piles of packages.

Crestfallen, I realized that Santa had not been able to find me. There was no gift beneath the tree from him for me.

I eyed the other bright parcels. "When can we open the presents?"

"Pretty soon," Mama said, the way grownups always do. "Grandmother and Grandfather are coming for breakfast. After that."

Sighing, I sat on the floor by the stove and sneaked a piece of candy. Georgie came out of his room looking sleepy. He poked me in the ribs, and I yelped.

"Merry Christmas, Kid," he said as he flopped into Grampa Ahbo's big leather chair.

When Grandmother and Grandfather finally arrived, Grandmother handed me a plate of cinnamon rolls to put on the table. Her eyes strayed to Grandfather every few minutes. He wore a suit, but it seemed too big for him. He was still pale, and now he walked with a cane.

After breakfast, everybody went into the front room where Georgie distributed the presents. I got checkers and some books and a doll cradle—from Grandfather! Surprised, I looked up at him.

"Did you make it?"

He nodded, smiling.

Everybody was thanking everybody else for gifts when Daddy said to me, "Chicky, what's in that package over by the piano?"

I stood up and looked. Sure enough, there was a big box wrapped in red paper with a note on it: "To Pat from Santa."

"He did find me!" I squealed, tossing ribbon and paper everywhere. Inside—wonder of wonders!—I found a shiny red dump truck *and* a blue steam shovel with a silver bucket scooper! Crowing with joy, I danced around, hugging everybody. Then I sat in the middle of the room, poured my marbles on the floor, and started scooping them with the steam shovel, dropping them in the truck bed, dumping them, and scooping them up again.

Georgie came over to help. Daddy joined us. Grampa Ahbo scooted his chair closer and leaned in, too. I was feeling kind of crowded when I looked up and noticed Grandfather. He was watching and looked sad. I got up and went over to lean on the arm of his chair.

"Do you want to play, too, Grandfather?" I asked.

"I'll just watch," he replied quietly.

"Thank you for the cradle," I said. "Did you really make it?"

He turned and smiled, right into my eyes. "Yes. Before I went to Portland." He reached over and smoothed my hair with his thin, white hand.

I watched the others playing with my dump truck, but I stayed there leaning on Grandfather's chair. I stayed a long time. That's where I wanted to be.

Christmas Sequins

by Judith Bader Jones

My stepmother wore a green suit that matched her emerald ring. Against my mother's advice, I had chosen an uncomfortable, but grown-up black sequined dress for Christmas dinner at Grandma and Grandpa Bader's farm, while my sister wore her pink cashmere sweater and Woolworth choker pearls. The car was cold and stuffy with cigar smoke as Daddy raced across the bumpy country roads.

When we reached my grandparents' farmhouse, snowflakes scurried about the back stoop. The wind whipped the heavy plastic tarp Grandpa covered the screen porch with in winter, making it crackle loudly in the intense cold. Hurrying inside, the delicious smells from the cookstove greeted us as we passed through the cold rooms, moving quickly toward the heated living room. I moved toward the modest circle of warmth that the grumbling oil stove in the corner sent out. Within the circle, Grandpa sat in a rocking chair. I sat on the scratchy horsehair couch nearby and felt goose bumps rise on my skin as the cold descended from the ceiling.

Grandpa looked at my father. "George B., how's business? Are you selling many John Deere tractors?"

"Business is good, Poppa," Daddy answered. "You ready to get a tractor?"

Grandpa shook his head. "Got a team of mules, don't need five-thousand-dollar tractors."

Quiet hung around the room as if there was nothing more to talk about except tractors, and Grandpa had stifled that conversation with his one remark. Uncomfortable, I glanced about the room. There was no Christmas tree, only a faded picture of Jesus hanging above the piano and a bowl of oranges strategically placed atop a doily on the table.

Uncle Winfield thankfully interrupted the silence. "Judy, want to walk to the barn?" I looked at my stiletto heels. He glanced at my feet. "I got army boots 'bout fit you."

He laced up the boots, and I quickly passed my stepmother's chair, noting the strange face she made and how her perfume seemed to follow us out the door. In the backyard, we stopped under the pecan tree. Uncle Winfield picked up one forgotten nut and handed it to me. "Your mama used to pick whole buckets of pecans out here," he said as I slipped the nut into my pocket, my teeth chattering.

Uncle Winfield must have realized my silky dress felt like a sheet of ice. He smiled. "Too bad you didn't wear warmer clothes. I wanted to take you to the river for cottonwood."

I glanced at my dress, now blotched with snow, wondering if it would leave a mark once it dried. I was dressed up—growing up—but something inside of me wanted to hang onto my childhood for one day longer.

"Do you have overalls in the barn?" I asked hopefully.

Within minutes, I was in the barn bunching up my dress and pulling on overalls and a jacket. I watched one sequin skitter to the floor. I left it there, a circle of glitter.

In the wagon, my thoughts moved to my uncle, who was duty bound to help his father farm river-bottom land, just as the mule team was duty bound to cart us through the snow. At the river, ice jiggled by, and my thoughts returned to myself. I felt like an ice castle forced to rush toward what lies ahead, overdressed for dinner, not dressed right for winter. Not ready, yet.

When we returned, Uncle Winfield wiped down the mules while I poked around the barn. Between the wall slats, I spotted a striped cat and three striped kittens. A fourth kitten, black with a tail tipped in white, appeared, and my heart melted.

Uncle Winfield smiled. "You take that odd-colored kitten home."

With the overalls on and the purring kitten close to me, I felt warmed from the inside out. I watched as the flickering light on the sequins caught the kitten's eye, and it batted playfully, bringing a smile to my face.

Once we were back in the house, I turned to my father. "Daddy, she wants to come home with me." He looked at me, then, as though he were looking at me for the first time all day. "George B, don't let her have that cat," my stepmother said. "Maybe we could get her a canary."

"You really want a cat?" Daddy asked, already knowing the answer. Suddenly, he smiled. "Well, why not. Girl needs a pet."

Grandpa nodded in agreement as the kitten purred contentedly in my arms.

When I returned to the home I shared with my mother and sister that night, I hung my dress in the back of the closet, put on pajamas, and sat in the living room by the fireplace with Mama and the kitten.

I looked at my mom happily. "I'll call her Sequin. What do you think?"

My mother wore her cozy quilted robe. She looked up from her book, smiled, and said, "That's fine. Was it cold on the farm?"

"It wasn't bad," I lied. Then digging in my pocket, I retrieved the pecan and handed it to her. "Uncle Winfield sent you something."

"He still has his old army boots," I added. "They're great in the snow. I wonder if the thrift shop has any?" I glanced at the fire and remembered my ride with Uncle Winfield. "You should have seen the river with the floating ice."

Mother turned the pecan over and over in her fingers. "Yes, I've seen the ice . . . something different about a farm at Christmas," she said wistfully, then turned toward the kitten and smiled. "I think that kitten is going to grow up a real city cat, but I doubt she'll forget her beginnings." She clutched the pecan in her palm. "I hope she doesn't grow up too fast."

## Make-Believe World

by Mary Jane Nordgren

Bill and Bob smelled of sweat and excitement, but then again, my teenaged uncles almost always smelled of sweat. It was the excitement that day, which caught my three-year-old attention—and that of my eight-year-old sister Carolyn.

As soon as Mom released us from the mandatory family greetings in Grandma's front hall in Mt. Washington, Pennsylvania, my sister and I tumbled under the mistletoe and into the living room. My eyes widened, and my sister and I stopped in our tracks as we looked at a room gone awry.

The sofa and two overstuffed chairs were crammed against the wall. Stands and tables were gone. Two-thirds of the twenty-by-twenty-foot living room floor was carpeted by a huge tarp laden with gleaming rails that circled and crossed and rose on a low ramp that bridged the tracks below and settled to the tarp just beyond a mirror lake. Mounds, blotched with browns and bearded with wisps of cotton, were studded with inch-high, green, tapered bristle-brush pines that poked their braided wire trunks into round green wooden bases.

Miniature cardboard houses and stores lined roads of fine gravel. Tiny pewter soldiers skated on the reflective surface of the mirror, and at the back corner, beneath the front window decorated with anchors to signify Uncle Bud's Navy days, a camouflage field extended up a papier-mâché mountain. And, if that wasn't enough, a gaping black arch loomed in the mountain.

It was magic!

"Looky here!" Carolyn exclaimed, beckoning me with those long slender fingers that knew every one of my ticklish spots. She danced around to the other side of the village with her back to the dining-room door. I scurried, squatting beside her to spy another dark arch.

"A tunnel!" Uncle Bob cried, brown eyes glittering in a flushed freckled face. "Wait'll you see!"

Both uncles flung themselves to the floor. Bill, dancing blue eyes intent under long lashes, rolled khaki sleeves up above his elbows before extending one lanky arm over the village store to throw a switch. Meanwhile, Bob lined up the middle of three control boxes.

"Ready?" Bob asked.

"Back 'er up a bit," Bill replied. "Yeah—there. *Now* we're ready."

Uncle Bob slithered to his right, and Bill flopped beside him, belly down on the magenta area rug.

"Slow and easy," Bill said with a conspiratorial smile. "Give 'em the full view first."

"Yeah," Bob grinned back.

Carolyn and I held our breath as brown fingers twisted knobs. And then, from deep within the black arch of the tunnel, a single dot of yellow-white light appeared and a low, piercing *wheeoooo* set the hairs on my arm tingling. I could hardly hear the train start over the pounding of my heart.

Suddenly, a sturdy black engine emerged from the tunnel like a retired master sergeant in stately parade. As the engine, with its tiny swinging bell atop, chugged forward, coal car, boxcar, low orange tender, and finally, the red caboose appeared.

I stood up and clapped chubby hands. And then, wonder of wonders, I saw a second beam of yellow-white light in the darkness of the tunnel! A second black engine emerged, pulling a work train. I fell forward on my knees, mouth agape, as the second train slowed and stopped on a thickened track near the water tower at the edge of the make-believe town, which my three-year-old mind believed was real. Never mind the uncle-size hands plunging into the tiny world to flip switches at the edge of my vision. When I saw the flatcar floor tilt and spill its cargo of logs near the water tower, I was sure a tiny engineer was responsible.

I grabbed at my sister's skirt. "Sissy, look!"

Carolyn chuckled through crowded white teeth. I knew as she twisted the ends of her honey-brown braids that she was as delighted as I was. When Carolyn knelt beside me, I spotted Uncle Bob scrunched between the mountain and the front wall. Bob was working feverishly at the other end of the mountain tunnel.

Another circle of bright light appeared! This time a sleek silver-gray engine emerged pulling streamlined silver passenger cars behind it. It was the prettiest train I'd ever seen, and I couldn't help myself. I squealed.

I sat down, cross-legged, trying to watch them all as each train rounded the widest oval then changed direction and sped off on different sets of tracks. I clapped my hands when the work train chugged up the ramp and crossed above, just as the red caboose of the first train skittered underneath.

Carolyn and I watched, mesmerized.

Our uncles kept glancing at each other, challenge mounting in their eyes. Bill repiled the logs onto the flatcar at the next pass around, then accelerated his train. First one and then the other, turning his respective dial farther and farther to the right. The trains gathered speed. When the sleek passenger train whooshed by—wobbling a pewter skater—Carolyn and I scarcely breathed.

One black engine roared under while the other roared over the ramp, each trailing a piercing *wheeeooo* as it tore up the track. The circuits grew faster; the misses narrower. The boys switched and shifted and reset tumbled cars after their engines flipped them from taking curves too fast. I hugged Carolyn, giggling and crossing my legs tight. I needed to go upstairs to the bathroom, but I couldn't leave.

Bobby had the work train scooting so fast that it whizzed on the inner figure eight. But even *his* huge brown eyes widened when he saw Billy lifting the passenger engine and setting it at the reverse end of the silver cars. Billy caught his brother's eye as he coupled the engine into place, grinning. Unless Bobby switched his tracks to keep both black engines from using that outer oval, eventually there would be a head-on collision. Bobby wiped his forehead and slowed his train, but he didn't switch the track. All four of us looked on with bated breath.

For that afternoon, my uncles were boys. Soon Bill would be "flying the Hump" over Burma, and Bob would be called into the Marine Corps between his last high school exam and the graduation ceremony. But for the moment, we chose to ignore the future, and with tiny wheels clacking and spinning, Christmas 1943, and our status as children in a make-believe world was preserved forever.

by Margaret Stanford Redmayne, as told to
Micheale Collie Shelton

**W**ar affects everything, even Christmas.

The Christmas of 1944 was bleak for everyone. Many of the ordinary everyday items, which we normally took for granted, were either rationed or not available. Families received Ration Stamp Books for meat, sugar, coffee, shoes, rubber, auto parts, and gas. There were few luxuries. In most areas of the country, in order to have vegetables year-round, families planted victory gardens. Once gardens withered up, families were left with nothing more than a hope and a prayer that the jars filled with fruits and vegetables in their pantries would last until the next growing season.

Since Harlingen, Texas, was located near the Mexican border, the climate allowed for fresh fruit and some vegetables regardless of the season, so families in this part of the country fared a bit better than families farther north. Still, luxuries were hard to come by, and one item that was in high demand everywhere was electric Christmas tree lights.

John and Margaret Stanford and their two-year-old daughter, Karen, lived in a small apartment just off Harlingen Army

Air Force base. John served as a gunnery instructor for the boys about to fly B-25s for bombing missions over Europe. During wartime, families were spread far and wide and were quick to bond with other families who also were far from loved ones. So when the Stanford family met Mary and Robert Browning and their teenage son, Tom, at church, they swiftly became good friends.

The Brownings had lived in Texas for a good many years and had a citrus grove, which helped keep the Stanford family in citrus fruit year-round. It also meant Karen would have an orange in her stocking, as was traditional in Winston-Salem, North Carolina, where the Stanford family had originated. Margaret and John were far from their home state and accepted the fact that many of the other traditional Christmas decorations were not at their disposal, especially such an extravagance as electric Christmas tree lights.

Despite the war, however, the Browning family had managed to hang on to their electric Christmas tree lights. As the holiday drew near, they invited their friends over for some Christmas hospitality. Their tree was a sight to behold. Little Karen, who had never before seen a Christmas tree with electric lights, was fascinated. Her blue eyes reflected the lights as she sat on the floor of the Brownings' living room, trying to reach up to each light.

The Stanfords returned the hospitality shown them and invited the Browning family over to see their tree. Margaret and John's tree was hung with homemade decorations and was beautiful, but it was not illuminated with the lights that had so captivated their young daughter on the Brownings' tree.

When Mary realized the Stanfords' Christmas tree did not have lights, she remarked that a child should have electric lights on her tree, noting that such a "wee one" was so impressed. Margaret insisted that would not be necessary. She felt their tree would be just fine for her daughter, who likely would not remember the Brownings' lit tree, anyway.

The next day, Mary and Tom knocked on the Stanfords' door. They had taken the electric lights off their tree and insisted they be put on Karen's tree. Margaret was taken aback by their generosity and questioned Tom. *Surely he wanted a beautifully lit tree?* He told her it would make him happier knowing that Karen would be able to gaze on the lights on her very own tree.

Mary also came bearing a request that John, Margaret, and Karen join them for Christmas dinner. Margaret was moved beyond words. Her family would have a beautiful tree and a fine Christmas dinner, thanks to the generosity of their friends.

Karen Stanford Shelton is in her early sixties now and is the grandmother to two wee ones of her own. She was so touched by the Brownings' generosity that Christmas day so long ago, that she has made sure this story was handed down in her family. Karen also makes sure that her grandchildren have a beautifully adorned—and lit—tree every year.

More than a Gift

by Nan Schindler Russell

$\mathcal{I}$ found nothing in the usual places. Would she hide it in the room I shared with my brother? I wondered, as my almost six-year-old hands dragged the straight chair across the wood floor. Standing tall on tiptoes, my fingers almost touched the knob above the closet door. Piling books on the chair, I climbed up again. This time, opening the cabinet that held extra blankets and family pictures, I found the shoe box.

Sliding the lid off, I spied blond hair. *Yes! Yes!* My heart raced. I was going to get a doll for Christmas. There she was. Everything I wanted. I visited Emma in her box whenever I could. I dared not pick her up or touch her; it was enough just to look at her. A week before Christmas, the rest of the family too busy with holiday tasks to keep close tabs on me, I positioned my makeshift ladder and expectantly opened the cabinet door. The shoe box was gone.

It seemed a long wait until Christmas morning when I spied the box under the tree, but it was worth it, knowing that Emma would be my doll forever. Although I realized Emma was the only gift I would receive, as I unwrapped the box my heart sang. Picking her up for the first time, now in a blue flowered dress with two other dresses lying beside her, I acted surprised to see her, and I knew my mother didn't suspect that this was not the first time we had met.

The year I found my only present is the year I found Christmas itself, although at the time, I didn't know it was happening. Cured from gift hunting forever, I remember my mother's face that Christmas morning. Love pouring from her eyes, excitedly watching her little girl unwrap her only present.

Years later, I learned how difficult a Christmas it had been for my parents. My father had been unable to find work, and our little family was far away from any of our loved ones. We had recently relocated to Arlington, California, for my brother's health. We were still reeling from a fire that six months earlier had destroyed most of our belongings when the woman in the adjoining duplex had fallen asleep while smoking.

With no money for presents, my mother had found the doll in a park a few blocks from our rented house a couple of weeks before Thanksgiving. The doll was abandoned, dirty, ragged, and falling apart. Mother had taken this thrown-away toy home and lovingly transformed and rebuilt her. She had even hand-sewn doll clothes late into the night out of my outgrown clothes.

My mother always says I didn't get anything else that Christmas, but she's wrong. I got more than Emma. I got the love that made her. Today, I don't remember Emma's face or what happened to her. But I still remember the love I saw on my mother's face that morning, and I still remember that it meant more to me then than any gaily wrapped gift that had ever come before it. And fifty years later? It means even more.

My Father

by Janet M. Hounsell
Conway, New Hampshire

N ow, in my twilight years, I find that my father, Vonley McAllister, is all wrapped up in my Christmas memories. Perhaps it's because he was born on Christmas Day, 1900; perhaps because once I reached adulthood, we exchanged weekly letters, and our Christmas gifts to each other were always checks for identical amounts. One year, he suggested we "cut down," since we'd both had unexpected expenses.

Or maybe it's because when he was recuperating from a serious operation and my mother—caring for her dying mother—could not accompany him, he loaded the car anyway, and drove sixty-five miles in a driving snowstorm to be with us.

That Christmas, which turned out to be his last, we hadn't expected him. We live in a resort community near the base of the Granite State's majestic Mount Washington. My parents lived to the north of us, and the route passed through a mountain notch road. It had snowed over a foot. The wind was blowing and visibility was practically nil. Our house was unusually quiet for a Christmas Eve, when suddenly, we heard a vehicle roaring and churning through the snow that blanketed our long driveway.

I looked out in amazement as Pop struggled out of his car and stepped into the snow, cigar clamped in his mouth, a bottle of wine under his arm. Tanya, his overweight dachshund, had to tunnel comically through the drifted snow and be lifted up onto the deck!

Puffing, Pop announced, "Wal, I guess I'm here for the duration, like it or not."

I smiled from ear to ear. The mischievous grin on my father's face reminded me of another Christmas when our two children were small. We could afford only one vehicle and that my hard-working husband used to reach his job, some distance away. We lived from one weekend and one paycheck to the next. That difficult year, on Christmas morning, my mother arrived alone with her car full of packages and foodstuff. I stared as she emerged from behind the wheel. *Where was Pop?*

Mother had more of a sparkle than usual as we hugged. She never could keep a secret, so she gave me an extra squeeze and whispered, "He's driving your present down, but don't tell him I let on!"

As we bustled through the cold into our house, I heard the phone ringing. It was Pop calling from a pay-phone booth. "Wal, Short Girl," he drawled, "you might want to be out in the dooryard. I'm driving my present up in a minute." That was all he said before he hung up. It gives me joy in my old age to think what a good time he was having at that moment.

Needless to say, we had formed a welcoming party in the snowy yard to greet him as he drove up. Pop, beaming, was at the wheel of a secondhand station wagon, honking the horn and twisting the wheel playfully.

Pop hadn't cashed in a bond or two to provide this gift; he'd amassed no such riches operating a village filling station. He had begun work as a mechanic's helper at age seventeen and had advanced to the position of chauffeur for a northern New Hampshire hotel by the time he married. He once explained it this way, "For some of us, the path of life is uphill all the way."

And the four-wheeled gift for his only child? Pop had searched for a promising much-used and affordable "set of wheels" as he always called a vehicle. Then he spent hours and hours, sometimes in twenty-minute snatches, improving it mechanically and cosmetically. It shone, inside and out. The gas tank was full; it had been registered and inspected; the windows gleamed; even the windshield wipers were new. And, Pop being Pop, it came complete with a tiny notebook full of nearly unintelligible information, the dates, cost of parts, time spent, and even items coded with the words "time left," were all noted when he felt the pressure of finishing by Christmas.

I will never forget that Christmas. The pure joy and pride on my father's face made that car the best Christmas gift a girl . . . full-grown or small . . . could ever receive.

# Spotlight on Conway, New Hampshire

---

## Town Facts

**Incorporated:** 1765
**Original name:** Pequawket
**Location:** Situated in the beautiful White Mountains of New Hampshire—the Granite State—the town of Conway is 339 miles from New York City and 131 miles from Boston, Massachusetts. Conway also lies close to the border of Maine and is a mere 62 miles from Maine's port city of Portland.

---

## Town History

Conway was named after Henry Seymore Conway, an English statesman and "prominent champion of the liberties of America." The town was incorporated in 1765, twenty-three years before New Hampshire became the nation's ninth state.

Conway is surrounded by the beautiful White Mountain Region on the foothills of Mount Washington (the highest peak in the northeast, at 6,288 feet above sea level), and consists of 1,040 acres, roughly in a six-mile-square. Within that space, Conway is composed of seven distinct villages, some with their own precincts and fire departments. The most notable of the seven villages is North Conway, which began early on to cater to tourism.

## Tourism

Beginning as an agricultural and lumbering community with many mills of various types, Conway has evolved into a town catering to tourism. The White Mountain National Forest is close by, and there are camping sites as well as many motels and hotels. The year-round population is 8,600, but many people own and maintain vacation dwellings in the area. The largest employer is Memorial Hospital in North Conway. Both Conway and North Conway have tasteful public libraries and plans for a new high school currently are in the works.

Because the area is mountainous, it seemed natural to cater to the skiing industry; it came as no surprise to the residents when North Conway became the town's center for downhill skiing, especially with the coming of the railroad. Today, North Conway proudly displays a prominent attraction—the restored Conway Scenic Railroad's unique 1874 depot. At the depot, tourists can take scenic rides and experience a taste of travel as it was long ago.

## Places to See

Conway's circa 1931 theater, the Majestic Theater, was recently damaged by fire, but it is slowly being restored to its original design. Conway village also has two attractive covered bridges that span the Saco River and the Swift River. The Saco River covered bridge is owned and maintained by the State of New Hampshire, and through a fundraising drive, the nearby Swift River covered bridge was saved from destruction and is now a "pedestrians only" span.

## Putting Conway on the Map

While tourism is what originally put Conway, New Hampshire, on the map, residents are quick to point out that actor Gordon Clapp, who played a prominent role in the television series *NYPD Blue* and won an Emmy Award in 1998 as Best Supporting Actor, was born in Conway.

In years past, the town also has had the opportunity to rub elbows with the late-great baseball star Babe Ruth, who often visited his daughter in North Conway. During his visits, he made friends playing golf at the North Conway Country Club, and residents remember him with fondness.

## Conway Today

Currently, Conway is poised to erect a new high school, which will also take tuition students from several nearby small towns. The older school, opened in 1924, will be thriftily recycled as a middle school.

Après ski and other lounges and many fine restaurants with varied offerings are spread throughout the town, which also is a mini mecca of outlet shops. Shoppers from cities in Massachusetts, Rhode Island, New Jersey, and elsewhere are in the habit of doing their "back-to-school" shopping in Conway. Prices are right, and shoppers can spend their saved money on attending summer theater shows or sending the kids to ice-skate at the Ham Ice Arena.

On a Wish and a Sled

by Joseph Pantatello

Christmas Eve—the year I turned six—was cold and snowy and would have been quite uneventful if it hadn't been for the Christmas tree. The Depression years were upon us and like everyone else, we were poor. Momma was busy in the kitchen preparing a special supper—a feast that I learned many years later had not come cheap—Papa had pawned the last of Momma's jewelry. To keep out of Momma's way, I tagged along with my older sister, Maria, when she insisted she had to go to confession.

On our way home from St. Francis church, we sloshed through graying snow, pausing to peer into storefront windows and making imaginary wish lists. A sled topped my list.

"Look at that coat," Maria whispered, cupping her hands on the glass for a better view. "A fur collar and a muff. I'd like that for Christmas, Joey." I looked at the coat and at all of the other items in the store window. I still held out for the sled.

As we stood there, the streetlights blinked on. Maria tugged at my sleeve. "Hurry, we can't be late. Papa will be home soon." I glanced at the trains in the window wistfully, but Maria had already begun walking. "Come on," she said, "we have four more blocks to go . . . and I'm getting cold!" She wrapped her coat tighter about her slender body as a gust of icy wind whipped around a corner.

As we trekked away from the busy thoroughfare, the sidewalk crowds thinned. On the next corner, we stopped to watch two men load Christmas trees onto a truck. One man wore a checkered mackinaw and was as big as Santa. The big man stopped what he was doing and glanced at me when I asked, "How come you're taking the trees away?"

"It's Christmas Eve, Sonny. Nobody's gonna buy a tree now," he replied.

I turned to Maria and whispered, "We don't have a tree."

I turned to the man, wide-eyed, and asked, "What's going to happen to all those trees?"

The man stopped loading, arched his back, and let out a low groan. "Gonna take them out to the beaches, keep the sand from washing away."

"We don't have a tree," I declared. My second Christmas wish, right under the sled, was that our family could have a Christmas tree.

"That's too bad, Sonny," he said as he heaved another tree onto the truck.

Maria frowned, grabbed my hand, and tried to pull me past the truck. I jerked away and returned to the back of the truck to stare at all of the beautiful Christmas trees. The sidewalk near the truck was littered with pine needles and broken branches, and the smell of pine, which reminded me of the way our house smelled when Momma cleaned the floors, filled the night air. The big man continued loading, his eyes never leaving mine. His gaze was so penetrating that it frightened me a little.

"I'm sorry that my little brother is bothering you," Maria said with an apologetic shrug. "He's just very inquisitive. He's going to school in January," she added. The big man smiled.

Maria bent down and looked me in the eye. "Joey," she said earnestly, "we have to go. I have to help Momma with the cooking. I promised."

Feeling as though a very important moment was passing me by, I watched sadly as the big man loaded the last tree—a scrawny six-footer with twisted limbs that needed a few more years in the forest. My feet stayed frozen to the ground as the two men picked up the broken branches strewn about and did their best to sweep away what remained of the glorious trees. I watched with a heavy heart as the other man climbed into the truck and started the engine.

My hope of having a Christmas tree disappeared as the big man hopped on the back of the truck and pulled a tarp over the trees. When he jumped down again, he turned toward me and grinned. His eyes glistened and he laughed one last time, his large belly rolling.

"I left you a small one," he shouted. "Merry Christmas!"

Maria and I hurried into the lot and found a blue spruce as tall as me, propped up against the one remaining stand. Light from the street lamp illuminated the area, turning the snow and ice-encrusted evergreen into the most beautiful tree we had ever seen.

"We have a tree!" I shouted, and embraced the tree, the pine scent filled my lungs and dislodged snow trickled down my back. "Maria, we have a Christmas tree!"

Maria grabbed the tree as I turned around to thank the man in the checkered mackinaw, but the truck had already moved out of sight. Turning back to my sister, I looked at our tree. It was small compared to the trees going to the beach, but it was full and thick, and even a six-year-old could see that we now had a problem.

My eyes filled with tears. "How are we going to get the tree home, Maria? We have a Christmas tree, and we can't even take it home!"

Maria did not answer right away. She was busy scanning the lot. Soon, she had scrounged up enough leftover twine to tie the tree to a beat-up cardboard box. Before long, she had fashioned a sled out of the flattened box and had lashed the tree to it. By tying the cord to one end, we found it easy to pull the sled along on the snow-covered sidewalk. I did not realize it at the time, but wishes really do come true. I had wished for a sled, and I had gotten one. It might only have been made of cardboard, but it was a magic sled, for without it my second wish might never have come true.

by Mimi Greenwood Knight

Just when I thought I'd explode if I waited another minute, I saw the school bus at the end of our road. The dogs saw it, too, and began to whimper. I had a surprise for my daughters, Haley and Molly, and had waited about as long as I could stand to share it with them. The bus slowed to a stop, and the girls leapt out. With a wave to the driver and a wild converging of dogs and kids, we began our familiar walk down the wooded driveway.

As they chattered on about things that had happened at school, I bit my lip and waited for my turn to tell them about the dilapidated box that sat in the middle of our living-room floor. I'd received a call from my aunt that morning, just after the girls had left for school. She told me she'd sold her house and was trying to empty the attic of four generations' worth of what she referred to as junk. While she cleaned, she found a box that had belonged to my parents. She didn't know what was in it or how it had landed in her attic, but wondered if I could come and get it. I'd burned up the road to her house to pick it up.

During my senior year of high school, my parents' house burned down. With it went all the photographs, heirlooms, baby books, and other family memorabilia. My aunt hadn't mentioned how old the box was, but I hoped with all of my heart that it was what my eleven brothers and sisters and I call "B.F." To us, "B.F." means treasures that were ours before the fire. Since my parents' deaths, any item that's "B. F." is priceless to us.

I told my girls about the box and that I'd waited to open it with them. They were as excited as I was! They loved stories about my childhood. My daddy was a Southern storyteller extraordinaire, and I suppose I inherited a bit of his talent. Haley and Molly can spend hours listening as I paint word pictures of my childhood summers along the Mississippi Gulf Coast and winters in the backwoods of Louisiana. The thought that they were actually going to see something—anything!—from my childhood was more than they could stand. We ran the last several feet to the house and gathered around the tattered box on the living-room floor.

I was vaguely aware of their voices as I pulled out a yellowed sheet of newspaper and read the date. January 14, 1977. Whatever it was, it was definitely "B. F." I picked up a crumpled bundle of newspaper so light that it felt empty. But, as I began to open it, I saw a half inch of brown paint and knew instantly what my cache held. I held it to my chest and felt my eyes brim with tears.

The girls squealed, "What is it, Mama? What is it?"

My throat constricted and the object in my hand grew wavy through my tears. I pulled the newsprint back on the worn figure of a shepherd. The top of his staff was missing and one foot was held on with yellowing glue. I laughed and cried as I carefully unwrapped the first tattered statues: Mary and Joseph. The three wise men, three shepherds, four sheep (one three-legged), a donkey, a cow with one horn, and Baby Jesus in his manger followed. Though I hadn't seen the statues in years, I knew every inch of them as well as I'd known Mama's hands and Daddy's laugh.

Haley could hardly wait for an explanation. "What is it, Mama?"

With eyes wide, Molly tugged at my sleeve, adding her own sense of urgency, "Tell us about it!"

I swallowed hard and began. "When I was Molly's age, your uncle Duff was away fighting in a war and couldn't come home for Christmas." Molly settled onto my lap and Haley stretched out on the floor turning one of the shepherds over in her hand. "It was the first time the fourteen of us wouldn't be together for the holidays, and my mother was exceedingly sad. One day just before Christmas, the mailman stopped at our house. Your aunt Michelle and I were playing in the front yard. He called us over and handed us a large package."

As I talked, my mind wandered back in time. It was December 1966, again. The trees hung heavy with Spanish moss. I could even hear our old dog Sarge barking at a squirrel he had treed. Mysterious nostalgia swirled about the room and feeling it, the girls snuggled in closer. They knew when moments like this descended, dinner and homework could wait.

I looked at them and smiled. "We couldn't imagine what was in the box. I saw that the stamps were in another language." In my mind's eye, I took the first steps toward the house. There was my mother at the kitchen window. Two of my brothers stopped tossing a football and ran across the pasture toward us. It was as if it was only yesterday.

I hugged Molly, gently rocking back and forth. "I remember Mama saying the box was from Duff and her voice cracking when she said it."

Haley's and Molly's eyes glazed over, and I knew they saw and heard it, too. I remembered the pictures that box had evoked for me of a place called Vietnam, a place I imagined so clearly when my father described it to us. Now, I wondered what pictures were emerging for my own little girls of the place where their mother grew up, of the people, the sounds, and the feelings of that day almost forty years ago.

Drawing a deep breath, I continued. "I sat in my daddy's lap and watched Mama place the figures in their stable for the first time. Daddy said that having them would be almost like having Duff home with us. That night, we sat beside the manger and sang Christmas carols into a tape recorder then took turns recording Christmas messages, which Daddy said he'd send to Duff, who he said was on the other side of the world. I fell asleep in Daddy's lap that night, staring at the figures by the light of the Christmas tree, listening to my mother's sewing machine whir in the next room and the older kids laugh over a game of Monopoly."

As I watched my young daughters examine the manger scene, I pulled the cardboard box closer to me. I ran my hand across the top of the box, fingering the ratty cardboard edges. Thirty-eight years ago, this very same box made its first journey across land and sea to bring a little piece of my brother home to the family that missed him. Now, it had traveled, again. This time the box traveled across time to bring my childhood and my parents to me. Through my father's gift of storytelling, the box also brought grandparents my daughters had never known or seen, into their home and hearts.

No Room for You, Either

by Dorothy L. Bussemer

It was Christmas week in Zanesville, Ohio, in the early 1940s—cold, dreary, and anxious.

On that particular morning, I had gotten off the bus at Fifth and Main Streets and noticed a group of people standing around the manger scene in front of the courthouse. The reason for this gathering was that the scene had been rearranged—a stray yellow dog had given birth in the middle of the manger.

What to do with the dog and her pups was the question on everyone's lips. The suggestions ranged from the ridiculous to the impossible. In my mind, the only sensible thing to do was to leave them alone and find something for the mother dog to eat.

The dog seemed anxious. I imagined she was wondering, in the way mothers do, how she could keep her babies warm enough, if she'd have enough to eat to supply the milk they needed, and above all, if her babies were safe in the presence of the crowd that had gathered.

My heart went out to her. She was doing the best she could for her family.

Just then, a truck pulled into the alley near one of the department stores and a man in the rough outdoor clothing of a farmer walked over and looked at the mother dog and her tiny puppies. He squatted down and petted the mother dog.

Keeping his tone quiet and calm, he said to her, "So there was no room at the inn for you, either."

He then removed his cap and placed the puppies inside, folding it over their small bodies to help keep them warm. I recognized the hat and scarf the farmer wore. One of his neighbors—Mrs. Gray, who knitted items for schoolchildren, and volunteer projects, such as the Red Cross war effort—had knitted the matching set for this particular farmer because he and his wife had always been so kind to others in the community. They always shared what little they had, and to show her appreciation, Mrs. Gray had also shared. I'm sure she never dreamed her gift would be used to cradle newborn puppies.

In the same calming voice, the farmer told the mother dog that he'd be right back. He then walked to his truck and deposited the puppies inside the warm cab. In a moment, he returned. Realizing the mother dog was too weak to walk, the man removed his scarf and wrapped it around her. Then he carried her to the truck to join her family.

As he prepared to drive off, he opened the truck door and called, "Merry Christmas and Happy New Year everyone!"

It was quiet for a few minutes after the farmer drove away. All of us—rich or poor, black and white, animal lover or not—were remembering another baby who was born in a manger because there had been no room for him, either.

When the news reached Mrs. Gray, she smiled and then put into words what the whole town was thinking. "That idea for knitting the hat and scarf must have come from God himself."

It has been more than fifty years since that cold day, but I think back on it often, for memories such as this make my Christmases very real, indeed.

## The Christmas Angel

by Trish Ayers

That morning, boxes filled with Christmas decorations were strewn across the floor in our little farmhouse. The melodic strains of Frank Sinatra's voice filled the room with Christmas melodies as I watched our dog Zack sniff the artificial Christmas tree, seemingly puzzled by its lack of smell, and my husband, Shan, artfully place the Christmas lights on the tree. Our youngest daughter, Ashley, was up in her room, but on hearing the sound of music drifting down, I knew she was awake. I went up to her room hoping to coax her downstairs so we could enjoy our family tradition of decorating the tree.

As I rounded the corner toward her bedroom, I called, "Ashley, the tree's up, Dad's put the lights on. Aren't you coming down?" I asked as I stepped into her room. I stopped in my tracks when I saw her wrapped up in her grandma's comforter, crying. *Was she remembering the past Christmases we'd shared with Shan's mom?* We all missed her, and holidays always seemed to bring forth memories of the times when she was still with us.

My heart went out to her. "Sweetie, what's wrong?"

Ashley looked up at me, her big green eyes glistening from the tears. "I hate Christmas. At least this year." Before I could say anything, she continued, "It's not going to be the same without Angela. Who's going to put the angel on the top of the tree? You know that's Angela's job."

*Ah, so that was it.* It wasn't bad enough to have one vacancy in the family tree this holiday season, her older sister, Angela, had opted not to come home for Christmas. This would be the first time one of my children would be missing, and it was obvious it affected Ashley tremendously.

I smiled sympathetically and sat down on the edge of the bed. "Ashley, we all miss your sister, but she's an adult now. She has her own life, her boyfriend . . . "

"She's forgotten us," pouted Ashley.

"You know that's not true," I said firmly. "There will come a time when you make the tough decision to not come home."

"No, I won't!"

For a moment, I sat there thinking about how much I, too, missed Angela. But, as a parent, I had to try and understand that each of our children must make her own way. It obviously was not that easy to accept for Ashley. I felt an ache deep in my chest as I patted my youngest daughter's arm consolingly, "You know, I miss her too."

Ashley must have noticed I was getting sad, for she changed the subject immediately.

"Is Mari up yet?" she asked.

Mari was the Japanese college student who was living with us for the year. The previous evening, we had told her about our tradition of decorating the Christmas tree. She seemed really excited about being a part of our American family custom.

Suddenly, the cheerful sounds of Mari playing downstairs with the dog drifted up the stairs. We smiled at each other, and Ashley released her hold on the comforter and jumped out of bed.

"I'm putting the angel on the tree!" She shouted and raced toward the stairs.

Within moments, the whole family was absorbed in the age-old tradition of decorating the Christmas tree. Shan picked an antique glass ornament that had hung on his family tree when he was a boy and placed it on the tree. And as Mari selected one ornament after another to put on the tree, Ashley followed her progress, explaining the memories associated with each. Though neither was fluent in the other's language, it was a joy to listen to them communicate.

As I bent down and examined the ornaments, my hand automatically reached for one of the angels. Ashley laughed, and then turned to Mari to explain.

"Mom always picks the angels," she said with a smile.

The morning stayed festive as we shared our memories with Mari. Even Zack picked a few ornaments, using his nose to point to them.

Once the familiar ornaments filled the tree, Shan stepped back and announced, "I think we're about done."

I looked at Ashley, smiled, and began to search for the angel tree-topper. It was carefully wrapped in the tissue paper that had surrounded it when my mother had mailed it to us so many years ago. Mom had spent hours creating the angel especially for our tree. I carefully handed the angel to Ashley, knowing this was an important moment for her. She smiled wide, then looked at the angel in her hands and turned toward Mari.

"The oldest daughter puts the angel on top of the tree at our house," she explained. "This was going to be my first year to place it there since Angela isn't here, but you're really the oldest," she said, offering the angel to Mari.

Tears filled Mari's eyes. "Are you sure, Ashley?"

"Yes," Ashley said with a firm nod.

As Mari stepped forward and placed the angel high on the tree, we were all moved to tears. My youngest daughter's act of kindness that morning served as a reminder to everyone in the room what Christmas is all about. Ashley had given Mari her finest gift, and she had done so willingly, straight from the heart.

Searching for the Holiday

by **Georgia Aker**
Rayo, New Mexico

It was a different kind of Christmas. There was no beautifully decorated tree with gifts piled under it. There was no turkey in the oven to be served to a houseful of guests. In fact, Dad and I were alone in our little adobe house. I had chosen to remain at home with Daddy when Mother and my brother Pat left to drive fifty miles away to spend the holiday at the home of my oldest brother, Vester.

Our home was one of a few simple homesteader shacks where ranchers eked out a living from the few cows this barren land would feed. Our family butchered a beef when needed and at least one hog each winter to provide us with ham, bacon, sausage, and lard.

There were no modern conveniences, and little communication with the outside world. We did have a post office where we got our mail on Tuesdays and Saturdays—if we wanted to ride four miles on horseback. There was a small in-home store, located about five miles from our house, but it was seldom open because ranchers usually had so little money to spend. Mother always milked one or two cows and kept a few hens, so we were seldom without milk, butter, and eggs. For staples, such as coffee, sugar, flour, canned goods, and feed for the cows, horses, and chickens, we traveled forty miles to Mountainair.

At Christmastime, the average high school graduate would have been dreaming of the attractions of an urban home bedecked with lights inside and out, and all the frills and thrills of celebration, but these thoughts weren't bothering me. I was too excited over something Daddy had said earlier that morning.

"Baby," he said, "you know Old Man Pulliam's saddle horse has been missing for several days. After breakfast, why don't we fix a lunch to take along, saddle our horses, and spend our day riding to see if we can find that horse? I know the Pulliams are away, but Mr. Pulliam is too old to go hunt the horse even if he were home."

We made a lunch we could carry on our saddles—sandwiches with home-cured ham and Mother's homemade bread, which we called light bread. We added a couple of slices of the cakes Mother had baked for the holidays, as well as an orange and an apple.

The day was not stormy, but cold enough that we appreciated the heavy coats we wore. I glanced over at my dad as the miles passed. I was proud to ride beside my cowboy father as we looked for the horse. And I was pleased to know that my dad was willing to consider the simple need of an elderly neighbor and to do what was necessary to meet that need.

# Spotlight on Rayo, New Mexico

---

### Town Facts

**Population:** 35

**Location:** Rayo is located in Socorro County, near the center of the state, about eighty miles from New Mexico's largest city, Albuquerque. It is within forty miles of Socorro, Belen, and Mountainair.

---

## History of Rayo

Settlers came into the area in response to the Homestead Act of 1862, which originally allowed U.S. citizens—twenty-one years of age—to apply for the right to settle on 160 acres of land. By meeting the requirements of five years of residency on the property, and the addition of certain improvements, the applicant was allowed to petition for a patent to the land. As the frontier moved to the arid land of the West, the amount of property was changed to 640 acres, and the number of years changed from five to three.

## Dust Storms Create Population Boom

During the Dust Storms of 1935, there was an increase in population in all of New Mexico, including Rayo. Numbers of people left Oklahoma for New Mexico, hoping to breathe better and to get a new start in ranching. Unfortunately, after they had sufficiently caught their breath, they began to realize the

640 acres would never be enough land to make a living for a family. Few were able to tough it out for the required years. Gradually, these nesters moved on to areas where they could find jobs and establish homes. This process has been repeated numerous times in the history of New Mexico's homesteading. In more recent years, people have finally learned, and ranchers have bought up these small holdings, either from the owners or from the government, and have built nice homes and made a decent living off the land. The Federal Land Policy and Management Act of 1976 ended homesteading.

## Early Transportation and Communication

According to Georgia Aker (Shaw), who lived in the area from 1916 until 1936, Rayo residents traveled either on horseback or in horse-drawn wagons. Later, most of the people depended on automobiles. Those who needed to travel by train could always flag down a train at Scholle, which was about twenty miles to the north, or head to Mountainair or Belen to the AT&SF train depot.

"There were no telephones; we had never heard of television," says Georgia. "A message might come through a neighbor who lived farther down the road and had stopped for a cup of coffee on his way home from Mountainair or Belen."

From 1916 to 1940, the community was served by an in-home U.S. post office, and mail was delivered on Saturday and again on Tuesday each week. Georgia's family happened to live closer to the post office than any of their neighbors, so it was understood that her family would pick up mail for all the people who lived south of their homestead. After Georgia's parents sorted out their mail, they put the rest into a big shoebox and placed it under their tall bedroom dresser. Neighbors knew where to find their mail. For instance, if John Adams came by when the Shaws weren't home, he would just twist the baling wire that held their front door shut, let himself in, thumb through the mail in the box, pull out his own, return the box to its place, and then go on his way. On occasion, he would take time to make a pot of coffee or look for some cold biscuits or leftover beans.

## Entertainment

Back in the day, when a Rayo resident decided to hold a shindig, they climbed onto the back of a horse and rode to all the ranches and gave word-of-mouth invitations. One such shindig was called a "Fruit Supper." Each of the men who attended the event brought a can of fruit, and the ladies brought their favorite home-baked cakes or cookies.

## Education

In the early years, Rayo had a one-room schoolhouse built out of rocks. Unfortunately, the school was used only for a few years, and today the rock walls have crumbled.

## Noteworthy People and Places

The renowned founder of Hilton Hotels, Conrad Hilton (December 25, 1887, to January 3, 1979), was born in the small town of San Antonio, New Mexico, about forty miles from Rayo. He studied at the New Mexico Institute of Mining and Technology in Socorro and at St. Michael's College, now called College of Santa Fe. Hilton began his career working in his father's store. He expanded the business and, after his father's death, began building a hotel empire, forming the Hilton Hotel's corporation in 1946.

## Rayo Today

The Rayo population is made up of the limited number of families who have bought the old homesteads. The average-size ranch in the area today covers approximately 30,000 to 40,000 acres. Families live in lovely modern homes, and the roads are in good shape, which makes it possible to travel to neighboring towns for supplies and entertainment. These days, personnel return to Rayo to a missile site that was erected in the 1990s, but they all exit again after the missile has been launched.

A Truly Memorable Christmas

by Sylvia Bright-Green

In 1953, just three weeks before Christmas, my dad was rushed to the hospital. In hushed tones, the doctor told my mom that if Dad did not have heart surgery, he would not live to see Christmas.

"Even then," the doctor explained, "his chances of surviving are very low. His heart is badly damaged."

Seeing the bewildered look on my siblings' faces, I knew I wasn't the only one who didn't understand what the doctor was saying. Our father was never sick, not even with a cold. How could this be happening?

As my thirteen brothers and sisters and I sat in the hospital waiting room, I wondered how long this was going to take. We had cows at home that would need milking soon. Thinking of those duties, I recalled how it was just yesterday that we kids had been making a list of what we were going to buy with our saved wages. Our plans were to purchase some items we had been coveting from the Sears & Roebuck catalog.

I planned to use my money to buy a pair of white figure skates. Some of my brothers wanted skis; another brother wanted a Lionel train set. My second-oldest sister wanted a guitar, and my two younger sisters wanted dolls that could drink and wet.

The money, and our yearlong desires for what we were going to do with it, gave us the incentive to perform our duties every day. It was those desires that made shoveling cow manure, slopping pigs, and milking cows at ungodly hours, and in all kinds of weather, more bearable.

I glanced at the clock on the hospital wall and was surprised to discover six hours had passed. Six hours that at first were filled with tears, then agitated pacing, and finally a silence so thick I could hear the ringing in my ears. Just when the ringing was reaching a fevered pitch, the surgeon appeared.

He looked around the waiting room, found my mother, and walked toward her. "Mrs. Bright," he said. "Your husband's heart is seriously impaired." He stepped closer to Mom and took her hand. "What I am trying to say is that I don't hold a lot of hope for him having a long lifespan. But God willing, I hope he does."

We all went into shock. *Was the surgeon saying Dad might die?*

During the ride home, no one said a word. When we entered the house and noticed how empty it was without Dad's voice filling the room, I started to cry. The rest of the family caught my tears. Huddling together to share our fears, Mom recited the Twenty-Third Psalm.

That night, before going to bed, we children held a meeting. We decided to use our money to buy Mom and Dad something they wouldn't normally buy for themselves. Paging through the hardware store's holiday advertisement, I suggested a 10-karat gold and black onyx ring for Dad and a delicate Bulova watch for Mom. My siblings agreed. And since, at sixteen, I was the oldest of the girls still living at home, I was elected to do the shopping.

The next day while Mom was at the hospital, our neighbor took me shopping. Standing at the counter waiting for my purchases to be packaged, my stomach was aflutter with excitement over my parents' gifts. When my best friend's mom, who clerked at the store, handed me my package, I wished her a Merry Christmas, hugged the bag to my heart, and left the store.

"Well, did you get what you wanted?" my neighbor asked as I floated toward her. I gave her a Cheshire cat smile and nodded my head. She flashed me a smile and then walked to the trunk of her car with her own purchases. When she attempted to open the trunk, it would not budge.

"Sylvia, can you help me?" she asked. "This gosh darn trunk has a habit of sticking in cold weather."

I immediately went to assist. After we finished putting her bags into the trunk, we drove away. I was anxious to get home. I could hardly contain my impatience to see the faces of my brothers and sisters when they viewed the gifts, and my parents' faces when they opened them on Christmas Eve.

My neighbor glanced over at me. "If you don't mind my asking, what did you get your parents?"

I reached down beside me on the car seat to retrieve the carefully chosen gifts, and then remembered.

"Stop the car!" I screamed. "I left my bag on the roof of the car when I helped you with the trunk!"

She quickly pulled over to the side of the road. I flung the car door open and leapt out, praying that the bag would still be on the roof. It wasn't. Horrified, I leaned against the car and sobbed.

We retraced our steps, searching everywhere, including the store parking lot, yet the bag was nowhere to be found. With a burdened heart and feeling like I had failed my siblings, not to mention my parents, I sobbed into my mittens. Between the tears, I silently begged God to return those gifts to us.

My neighbor, seeing how distraught I was, offered to come into the house to explain. The moment we entered the house, my brothers and sisters came rushing toward us.

"Dad's coming home for Christmas!" my oldest brother announced cheerfully. He held up a package and smiled. "The gifts you picked out and had the store deliver are perfect. This truly is going to be a memorable Christmas!"

And it was. I hadn't asked the store to deliver the package, and no one knows exactly how the gifts made their way to our house that day. But we do know that our family had been chosen to receive a Christmas miracle.

Scarves and Popcorn

by Sandra McGarrity

"It's colder out here than I thought it was going to be," Mother declared, a small frown creasing her forehead. "I can't believe we forgot your caps."

My two sisters and I stood on the sidewalk beside Mother, happily chattering away while she worried. We weren't concerned about our heads. To dispel the cold, we stamped our feet energetically and enthusiastically. We were having a great time.

Dazzling Christmas decorations embellished the full length of Main Street. The huge tree in the Court Square was decked out with hundreds of ornaments and draped all around with silver tinsel. The store windows displayed treasures of bicycles and baby dolls that made us giddy with excitement. We joyfully embraced the magical world of colored lights and candy canes that surrounded us.

It seemed as if the entire population of our small town lined the street waiting for the Christmas parade. The annual parade was an important event in our lives, and few people missed it. This particular parade was to be the best one ever because our older sister, the fourth "stairstep" was riding on one of the floats. It wasn't just any float, either. She was riding on the main one—the one with the big guy in the red suit. Our sister was to be a part of the grand finale as one of Santa's helpers. For this day, she was one of the most important people in the town. We were her sisters, so that made us pretty important, too.

Mother shook her head in self-reprimand and added, "I don't need a house full of sick children." Then she squinted up the street, her face laced with concern. "Pat is already probably freezing to death, riding that float dressed in pajamas. I can't let the rest of you freeze, too."

In truth, there was no way that we could be freezing. We were tightly bundled against the winter day in pants, heavy socks and shoes, coats, gloves, mittens; you name it. It was just that somehow, our caps had been forgotten. As about the most conscientious mother on the planet, our mother stood there convincing herself that we would be fatally ill before morning if she allowed our heads to go uncovered.

Gail, Debbie, and I continued to talk and giggle. We craned our necks, hoping to catch a glimpse of the police car that would begin the parade. We weren't at all concerned about our cap-less state. We just wanted to see the parade. But Mother had other plans.

In the next instant, Mother had pulled out her coin bag, counted the change, then dug to the bottom of her purse and found a few more coins. She counted the coins one final time, and then looked across the street to the dime store. She cast a furtive glance up and down the empty street. "You three stand right here and don't move. I'll be back in a few minutes."

The Christmas spirit, as well as three little hearts, began to sink within us. She had that determined look on her face. We clamored around her. "Where are you going?"

"I'm going to the dime store to buy some headscarves," she spoke firmly. "You are going to get sick without your heads covered."

We groaned in unison. "We don't need scarves!" We whined and complained as much as we dared. Horrors! It was 1959, almost 1960. Girls didn't wear headscarves! Scarves were for old women like our grandmother and for very poor people, who couldn't afford the cute little knitted caps that we had left at home. Was she really going to do this to us?

Without a moment's hesitation, she marched across the street and disappeared into the dime store. She was a woman on a mission. Her mind was made up. There was no stopping her. She was going to do it, and worse still, we were going to wear them.

We stood on the sidewalk and discussed our fate. We were going to look so stupid. What if our school friends saw us? Tears welled in our eyes as we mourned our unhappy circumstances. We folded our arms tightly around our bodies and pouted while we watched the storefront for her return. In view of our eminent fall in society, window displays didn't seem to glitter as brilliantly as they had before. It was as if someone had turned on a dimmer switch. Why did our mother have to be so . . . so . . . motherly?

Within ten minutes, she emerged from the store with a bag containing the hideous headgear that would undoubtedly seal our fate. People were going to think that we were . . . poor. We were going to look like little waifs. Didn't it bother her that her children were going to look like street urchins?

But, wait. She had something else in her hands. It looked like . . . could it be? Yes, it was! She carried three bags of hot buttered popcorn, fresh from the dime-store popper! This was an almost unheard-of treat. The pouts turned to smiles. The glimmer returned to our world. Surely, our town had never before boasted such brilliant holiday decorations, nor had the winter air ever had such a clean, fresh snap to it.

As we watched excitedly, Mother hurried across the street and then handed a bag to each of us. While we dove into the buttery goodness that she'd brought to soften the blow, she tied a scarf around each of our heads. Just as she securely knotted the last scarf under my chin, we heard the blast of the siren from the police car. The parade had begun.

We were near the bottom of the popcorn bags when the final float came into view.

Dressed in her costume of a red-and-white striped pajama top, with red pants and an elf cap, our sister rode proudly beside Santa. We made certain that anyone within a mile's radius of us was aware that our sister was on that float.

Beside us, Mother wrapped her fingers around her purse and glanced at her family, the touch of a smile on her lips. Inside her purse was a now-empty coin bag, but her eldest daughter was a celebrity for the day, and her three younger daughters were warm and snug under headscarves that they no longer remembered they were wearing. She straightened her shoulders proudly. She knew when to spend her last coin.

# Poke-and-Plum Town

by Marilyn Jaskulke

It's been said, "If you poke your head out of the car window while driving twenty miles an hour, in less than a minute, you're plum out of town." At two blocks wide and about as narrow, Northrop, Minnesota, which maintains a steady population of around 200 folks, fits the description of a poke-and-plum town.

For the fifty-three years Hubby and I have been married, the number of people hasn't changed much. But other things certainly have.

One thing I will never forget about the earlier Northrop is how the church bells kept the community informed. Reaching all four corners of town, tolling church bells sounded for Sunday services, funerals, and weddings. When a parishioner died, the bells rang the number of times that matched the age of the deceased, and the whole town stood still to count and ascertain who might have passed on. Wedding bells resounded with a mellowness that differed from all the rest.

When we decided to tie the knot, there was no doubt about where we would get married, but why I chose December 25 as my wedding date remains a mystery. Certainly, it would be a date that no one would ever forget. Maybe that was my plan.

"We will need a rehearsal," our pastor said when I told him of the date.

"It'll be small," I answered, shaking my head. "We won't need a rehearsal." I didn't attempt to explain that my parents had said no to a costly wedding, nor that my future husband had told me that he would *not* wear a tux.

So on December 25, 1951, when the pastor trudged through the snow from the parsonage across the street to meet us at the church, the only ones present were the bride and groom and our two families. In minutes, we were reciting the vows that would remain sacred to us for the rest of our lives.

When it came my turn, I answered loud and clear. I don't remember my spouse being as adamant with his wedding vows as he had been about the tuxedo, but in my opinion, fifty-three years together is proof of the pudding! For some reason, no church bells peeled for our small gathering in Northrop, Minnesota, that day. Perhaps the pastor wanted to get back home to his family Christmas and didn't feel like climbing the stairs to the bell tower. At the time, Hubby and I were too busy to pay it much heed. Instead, we climbed into his new green 1949 Chevy and scooted through that little poke-and-plum town to a nearby photographer for our wedding picture.

On our way, we caught glimpses of smoke curl from chimneys in homes where families were gathered to celebrate Christmas Day, and I smiled contentedly. Bright red and green Christmas tree lights reflected from windows that shimmered behind a frosty glaze. In the magic of the evening, the houses seemed to glisten like the tiny holiday village that sat on a fluff of cotton on top of my mother's piano. On the opposite side of the street, children whirled and twirled on the summer baseball field that had been turned into a winter skating rink. The skaters wore warm and cozy colorful new Christmas mittens and tasseled stocking caps that had been simple Christmas packages beneath the tree only the night before.

That was so long ago, but I remember it like it was yesterday. We were married in a poke-and-plum town, on Christmas Day, and it worked to our advantage, for we have been blessed beyond all measure.

These days, sweet nostalgia skates through my mind when I hear the first carols of the season. I remember our first Christmas tree with bubble lights that danced and gurgled, the popcorn and cranberries we'd strung, and our commitment to a new life together. Though we exchanged no Christmas gifts on our wedding day, we received the kind of gifts that can't be wrapped in paper or ribbons: our love.

# The Great Walnut Caper

by Catherine Lanser

*I*'ve heard people say that Christmas today is busier than it was when they were young. Having grown up in a family of nine kids, I disagree. In our family, the months before the holiday were frantic. On top of shopping and baking dozens and dozens of cookies in every shape, color, and flavor, my mom started a tradition of making keepsake ornaments for each child. Her plan was to give us enough ornaments to decorate our own Christmas tree when we left home. Even though I didn't appreciate them then, these ornaments have become my most treasured memories.

Mom didn't hide the ornaments, but the cookies were always hidden in the attic. It was as cold up there as the Wisconsin winter, so they stayed fresh until Christmas Eve. My brothers, sisters, and I knew her hiding spot and snuck up there for a cookie buffet every time she and Dad left the house. Occasionally, Mom would hear the attic door closing as she entered the house, but we denied our involvement even as the cookie crumbs fell from our sweaters.

One year, Mom made ornaments that looked like strawberries. She used whole walnuts and created them in a simple three-step process. The first step was to paint the walnuts red. After they dried, she painted black dots to resemble seeds. Finally, she glued green felt leaves to the top and attached an ornament hanger. In between coats of paint she would let them dry on a sheet of newspaper under a chair in the living room. She worked steadily toward Christmas, and everything was progressing smoothly, until the walnuts began to disappear.

The first day, she didn't say anything. Even though she remembered putting them under the chair, she doubted herself and thought—perhaps—she had misplaced them. She painted a few more walnuts and placed them under the chair to dry. When they were missing again the next day, she had a pretty good idea where they went. She pointed her finger at her three youngest children. The only ones without a job, we were the ones she figured were desperate enough to steal painted walnuts. She summoned Tommy, Pattie, and me to the kitchen table and began her interrogation.

"I put painted walnuts under the chair last night and when I got home from work today, they were gone," she said. "What happened to them?"

We three looked at one other. I knew I hadn't done it. I sat back waiting for one of the others to confess.

"Wasn't me," Pattie said.

"I didn't even know where they were," said Tommy.

"Me either," I said.

"Well, I guess they just got up and walked away," Mom replied.

She left the room and spent the rest of the evening painting new ornaments. The next morning, she looked under the chair just as she was about to leave the house for work. She grunted in disgust.

"You kids," she said loudly, as she opened the front door. "I'm going find out who did this when I get home!"

"Did you guys do it?" Pattie asked my brother and me as Mom closed the door. Tommy and I shook our heads.

Before dinner, we were summoned to the kitchen table again.

"Which one of you ate my walnuts?" She asked, determined to get to the bottom of this mystery once and for all.

We shook our heads and denied any involvement. We had spent the hour between the time we got home from school and the time she got home from work pilfering cookies in the attic, but we hadn't eaten any walnuts.

"I'll find out who it was," she said.

That night, she painted more walnuts and carried them to her bedroom. She hid them under her bed where we wouldn't dare steal them. The next morning, she led us down the hallway to show us her new hiding spot.

"Now we'll see if you took them or not," she said. "I hid them here last night where you wouldn't find them. If they're still there, I guess I know it was one of you."

She lifted up the bedspread, and we leaned over to inspect the sheet of newspaper. There were no walnuts, just red circles of dried paint where the walnuts had been.

"Oh, come on," she said. "Which one of you is eating my walnuts?"

We looked at each other again and shook our heads. We knew the crimes we were guilty of and stealing walnuts was not one of them. With a whole attic full of Christmas cookies, the thought of plain walnuts seemed pretty boring.

Tommy knelt down and put his face under the bed. "I think I know who took your walnuts," he said.

"Who?"

"We have mice," he said pulling the newspaper from under the bed and revealing tiny red footprints leading across the newsprint.

Mom pulled the newspaper toward her face. "Well, sure enough, that solves it," she said. "I'll have to hide them higher tonight."

She walked to the hallway closet and pulled down her box of craft supplies. She painted a new group of walnuts red and put them on the top closet shelf. The next morning we waited as she opened the closet door, revealing the red walnuts she had created the night before. After that, there were no more missing walnuts. She finally finished them the night before Christmas Eve.

"What do you think?" she asked, holding up a completed ornament.

"Nice," we said.

That night she announced that she was going to put together some cookie plates for the neighbors. Then she asked Pattie to pull down the attic steps.

"I made some Christmas cookies, and you can all help me." She said it as if we didn't know the cookies were there . . . as if we hadn't been sampling them for weeks. We carried the containers to the kitchen table, exchanging guilty glances. Mom opened them one by one and shook her head at the now half-full containers.

She sighed. "I guess we have mice in the attic, too."

**Christmas Blues**

by Kathe Campbell

𝔍f you have married children, you most likely have been a part of the parent-juggling that takes place each year for the holidays. I call it the Every Other Holiday Syndrome— wife's parents on odd years, husband's family on even years. Simple, really, and understandable, except that one Christmas when unforeseen circumstances found us facing our first holiday alone.

We could have handled it—and would have—if our golden retriever, Nikki, had not collapsed and forced Ken and me to say goodbye to our beloved lady. We were heartsick over our loss. I cried buckets while Ken labored to keep his macho image intact. Finally, he, too, let go. It was a dreadful scene.

A week later, severe arthritis and profound loneliness for Nikki, rendered our fifteen-year-old Border collie, Ginger, withdrawn, incontinent, and unable to walk. The excruciating trip to the veterinarian to put our second dog to sleep was nearly more than we old souls could handle. Ginger had been what we mountain folks call a *dump-off,* and we had gladly adopted this sweet and loyal herder.

On Christmas Eve morning, Ken popped out of bed full of oats and vinegar. I, on the other hand, was still caught up in gloom and despair over beloved dogs and slightly miffed at his seemingly joyous attitude.

"I'll be back in a while, dear," Ken shouted on his way out the door.

As the rising sun's radiance surfaced the top of our mountain, I stood at the window attempting to pull myself together. I yearned for the joyous sound of grandchildren to take away the deathly quiet that now filled our home.

Around noon, Ken drove in through the front gate. As soon as he opened the truck door, a tricolor blob of fur flew out. I watched in amazement as a ten-month-old keeshond (Dutch barge dog) that had been relegated to the Humane Shelter raced through the snow onto the deck and into my outstretched arms. We fell over in a joyous heap of emotion, this medium-size, curly-tailed bundle of yips and slurps, and me. Ken explained that she was the sorriest-looking pup in the place and her brown eyes had pleaded, *"Please, Mister, take me home with you."*

I could tell by the look on his face that he was smitten. And so was I.

Like two old fools, we took Keesha to town for a lovely Christmas Eve dinner with us. Keesha's was in the form of a doggy box. Then we went to Wal-Mart to choose all the right toys and the perfect collar. Keesha readily stuck her nose up at silly toys. Her passions were in a different direction. She wanted to be talked to often, to sit close to us, to work hard, and to receive unconditional love.

Early on Christmas morning, we watched the newest member of our family play in the snow and get to know the donkeys, ducks, geese, and cottontail rabbits. Gratefully, she had no desire to torment the other creatures.

She was a keeper.

And, so, instead of hanging around pretending we weren't sadly devoid of human companionship, we grabbed Keesha and headed for our Salvation Army Church headquarters.

Along with other volunteers, we served ham and turkey dinners to a dining room overflowing with humble families. The homeless, alone and destitute, had gathered to dine in the shadow of Jesus' house. As we looked around, Ken and I both felt a tad ashamed of our own holiday blues.

That evening, we returned home bone-tired but elated. We were greeted by hungry waterfowl and four-legged creatures lamenting their late Christmas fare. We smiled at each other as Keesha added her bark to the chorus. Though our work was far from over, this day would go down in our memories as the most blessed of Christmases.

From the Heart

by Joyce Anne Munn
Sciotoville, Ohio

When I was a child, my family didn't have money for many Christmas gifts. I always knew, though, that two special presents would be under the tree: a jigsaw puzzle and a doll. The year that I was eleven was no different. I shook the rectangular box to make sure and held the other box carefully, wondering what to name the yet unseen doll.

We had opened our gifts early that Christmas Sunday morning, and my new doll had already found a place of importance in my heart. Before Daddy left for his church bus route, we had assessed the difficulty of the new puzzle and when we might start assembling it. Daddy asked what I had named my doll, but I just shook my head as I had made no decision yet.

A short while later, I heard Daddy return from the bus route and knew that soon I would have to stop playing with my new doll and get ready for church. I looked up at my father as he walked into the house and gasped, my new doll falling from my hands.

Daddy was crying!

I had never experienced this. *What was wrong?* He called for Mother and motioned for me to sit with him on the couch.

Quietly, he explained that on his bus route that morning, he had seen the house of a rather poor family burned to the ground. The family had lost everything.

He looked at me and spoke slowly and deliberately, "I saw a little girl about five years old. Everything she had is gone."

His heart communicated with mine. I knew exactly what he wanted without hearing the words. I got up and walked to where my new—yet unnamed—doll had fallen. I picked her up and handed her to Daddy. As he hugged me, I felt fresh tears on his cheek.

"We'll take her to the little girl after church," he said, quietly.

As we pulled up to the burned out house, I gasped at the horrific sight, imagining how it would feel if it had been my own house. Several people were poking through the rubble; all were withdrawn and silent. We climbed out of the car, and I held tightly to my new doll as Daddy gently guided me toward a little girl standing off to one side. As we neared the sad-faced child, my grasp on the doll lessened. It took only a couple of seconds for me to hand her the doll. She reached out and clasped the gift tightly against her body. A slight smile crossed her face. In that instant, I knew I would not miss this doll. Others were waiting for me at home.

Over the next few years, if I saw a house fire or read about one, this particular fire, the little girl and my doll briefly came to mind. Fourteen years later, however, when I was twenty-five. I was to learn more of the story, and from that day forward it would remain fresh in my mind.

When my father died suddenly, unexpectedly, I flew across the country to my hometown, treasured memories flitting in and out of my distraught mind. Although many special Christmas memories crossed my mind, I honestly don't think the year of the fire was one of them. Instead, I recalled the special times of decorating the tree as a family or visiting with nearby relatives.

But on the day of Daddy's funeral, just before it was time for the service to begin, a strange thing happened. A young lady walked up to the casket and stood there sobbing. After a few minutes, she came up to my mother and hugged her.

"I loved him like a father," she said softly. Then she turned and walked out.

I was baffled. *Who was this stranger?*

After the funeral, I turned to Mother, "Who was she?" I asked.

Mother smiled. "Do you remember the Christmas of the fire?"

As the story unfolded, I nodded slowly, absorbing a new understanding of who my father had been. The young woman's name was Barbara. She was the girl who had received my Christmas doll so many years before. Over the years, she had stopped by to visit my dad at his gas station. He had helped her family more than I knew, and, I discovered, he had also had helped others in much the same way.

That year, Christmas was different for me. My eyes were open to those around me who were in need. Daddy's concern for others became my view, too. I scanned newspapers and listened to news reports about home fires during the holidays. Though I always hoped my search would come up empty, from time to time, I've had the opportunity to help such families.

I've also come to realize that many needs exist even without the destruction of a fire to contend with. Being able to give special Christmas gifts to those in need has been a way for me to honor Daddy's memory. By his actions, my father taught me that the love that describes the season is a love that can be passed on and on and on, if we but give from the heart.

# Spotlight on Sciotoville, Ohio

Town Facts

**Population:** 4,000

**Location:** Sciotoville is located on the Ohio River, 120 miles east of Cincinnati and 90 miles south of Columbus.

## An Unofficial Town

Today, the town of Sciotoville, Ohio, exists only in the hearts and minds of residents who currently live within the city limits of Portsmouth, Ohio, population 19,500. Sciotoville lost its official identity in 1921 when it merged with the city of Portsmouth. As the story goes, Sciotoville and New Boston, both small towns, were to merge with Portsmouth. As the merger date drew nearer, New Boston pulled out of the deal. At that point, Sciotoville leaders took a closer look at what the merger would mean to them, and they, too, attempted to withdraw. Unfortunately, it was too late. The merger went through, and for all intents and purposes, the town known as Sciotoville was no more. But old habits die hard, and the residents, exceedingly unhappy about the merger, did not concern themselves with the fact that their town would no longer appear on the map. They have continued calling their neck of the woods Sciotoville, and it doesn't appear to have harmed anyone. Even mail addressed to Sciotoville residents arrives at its destination. Today, the community has their own high school named Sciotoville Community School, but commonly referred to as East High School.

## Business and Industry

Until the decline of the railroad industry, three major rail lines—the Chesapeake & Ohio, the Norfolk & Western, and the Baltimore & Ohio—passed through the area, employing many local residents.

The Detroit Steel Company had a huge mill in town and was the major employer until economics also closed its doors. Additionally, two major shoe companies, Selby and Williams, also had large work forces in the area until the '50s and '60s. When these big companies shut their doors, many people were forced to move in search of employment. Today, like many small struggling towns, city officials are working hard to entice industries and businesses to return to the area. Sunoco Chemicals has been a source of employment for many years, and Ohio's youngest four-year college, Shawnee State University, is doing much to improve the economy.

## Places of Note

The Shawnee State Forest, some 65,000 acres of picturesque hilly land that was once the hunting grounds of the great Shawnee Indian tribes, now provides nearly fifty miles of hiking trails for the area's many visitors.

## Floodwater Mural Depicts Rich History

Because the town is located on the Ohio River, in the early 1900s spring flooding was a way of life for area residents. After a particularly damaging flood, the existing 2,000-foot long, 20-foot high floodwall was built to protect the area from further damage. Then in the 1990s, artist Robert Dafford was commissioned to paint the area's history on the floodwall.

Ever since he began, thousands of visitors have traveled to the area each year to relive local Ohio history with its residents. The mural depicts the Shawnee Indians as they were in the 1700s, and moves up through history to the present, including well-known people and groups from Portsmouth. The dedication panel was completed in 2002. One of the most popular areas of the floodwall is the part that includes a picture of Roy Rogers mounted on his horse, Trigger.

## Famous Residents

Though Roy Rogers (Leonard Slye) was born in Cincinnati, Ohio, his family moved to the Portsmouth area in a home-made houseboat, when he was a small child. The family lived aboard the boat for several years, making the Ohio River their home. Shortly after, the family secured the boat on land and prepared it to serve as their permanent dwelling but a flood swept the houseboat away. It wasn't long afterward when the family moved to the country. When Roy was eighteen years old, he moved to California. An area of downtown is named the Roy Rogers Esplanade.

## Sports Trivia

In 1934, due to the Depression and sad economic state of the country, the Portsmouth Spartans, an early NFL team, became the Detroit Lions. Additionally, Branch Rickey, born and bred in the Portsmouth area, coached a baseball team known as the Portsmouth Redbirds in the early twentieth century. Also, in 1927, near the end of Jim Thorpe's career, much to the enthusiasm of his fans, the legendary player became a coach and coached the Shoe-Steels, a semipro football team.

The Half-Priced Puppy

by Joyce McDonald Hoskins

Traditionally, Christmas is supposed to be the happiest time of the year. But what if it's not?

I was thirty-nine years old before I experienced my first sad Christmas. In 1983, my father died four days before the holiday. He had cancer. The doctors had said he had five good years. The reality was five months.

Leaving my husband and son behind in sunny Florida, I boarded a plane and flew toward a bleak West Virginia winter to say goodbye to my father for the last time. All around me there were people laden down with packages, smiling. I sat in my seat with a heavy heart. As the plane inched closer to my home, the tears rolled down my face.

On Christmas Eve the following year, I drove into town to do some last-minute shopping. As I headed toward my car, memories of the previous holiday flooded my heart, and tears threatened. The stores were beginning to close when I spotted a new pet store. Feeling sentimental, I thought of how much my ten-year-old loved guinea pigs.

"Welcome to Stuart," I said to the lady behind the counter. She smiled and in seconds we had struck up a conversation. I scanned the pet shop as we talked. The store had the Christmas Eve look—picked over.

"No guinea pigs?" I asked hopefully.

"Sorry," she answered.

"Hmm, well, I'll bring my son by after the holidays," I said. "He loves animals."

As I started to leave, I heard a whimper and looked around. For the first time, I noticed a tiny black puppy in the shadows in the back of one of the cages. As the puppy whined again, I recalled the vow I had taken to never own another dog. Fleas were just too hard to contend with in Florida. But, fleas or not, I couldn't resist the urge to hold the puppy for a few minutes.

The lady took the puppy out of the cage and placed her on the counter. In less than a minute that tiny poodle managed to lick her way into my heart. I thought about the $50 bill I had in my purse, the last of my Christmas shopping money, and frowned. It certainly wouldn't be enough to buy a registered poodle.

"Toy poodle?" I asked.

"Yes."

"Papers?"

The woman nodded. "And fifty percent off."

Right, fifty percent off $300, I thought. Looking back at the pup, I asked, "How much would that be?"

"Fifty."

I turned toward the shop owner with wide eyes. "Only fifty dollars?"

She nodded again and scratched the dog's head.

"Tax?"

"Included."

While I thought about it, I pondered aloud. "I'd have to buy food."

"I'll give you enough to get you through the holidays," she said quickly.

I hesitated. There were a million good reasons I shouldn't have the puppy, but it was Christmas Eve, and that puppy sure felt good in my arms. And right there on impulse, I did what all pet experts advise you not to do—I bought the puppy.

As soon as I climbed back into my car, the puppy wriggled loose of my arms and jumped up onto my shoulders. It probably wasn't safe, but she rode in the car between the headrest and my shoulders every time she got in the car for the next fourteen years.

They say you can't buy love, but I don't believe it. I think you can. Sometimes it even comes half-price.

The Christmases of My Youth

by Charlotte A. Hilliard

The Christmases of my youth were spent in joyous celebration of the birth of Jesus, with long nights watching *Amahal and the Night Riders* on the television, and the *Bob Hope Armed Forces Christmas* specials. What a difference from the high-priced holiday we celebrate today.

Growing up, when the first of December rolled around, excitement rose in me like sap in a sugar maple. The first gifts were Sears & Roebuck Co. and Montgomery Ward Christmas catalogs. Every picture on every page was analyzed and memorized.

"Take this pencil and mark the things you like most with a great big *X*," Ma Peal told me.

Everything got penciled, except stupid boy things. The most marked-up baby doll in the book was all Santa picked from the catalogs, but that was okay. People ordered what they had money to pay for, and that was not much. Looking at, wishing for, and dreaming about the wondrous things found between the covers of that catalog were almost as much fun as unwrapping presents on Christmas morning.

Early on, I began bugging Ma Pearl and Pa to get a Christmas tree. I knew the answer would always be—wait. We compromised. Though it was never soon enough, eventually it was time to get the tree. Each year it was the same ritual. Our tree was always a cedar, much larger than needed.

Deciding what tree we ended up with was a lengthy and mentally challenging task.

"Pa, here's a pretty one. Let's get it," I'd shout.

"Okay, if you're sure, we'll cut it down," he'd answer.

Looking around, I would soon spot another tree—one that looked even better. "No, wait," I'd say, "Let's look at that one. I think it's prettier." Then grabbing my mother's arm, I'll haul her along. "Come on, Ma Pearl, let's go look at it."

"I'm coming," Ma Pearl would answer. "Slow down!" When she finally stood in front of it, she would smile. "It is pretty." Then she'd turn to Pa. "Brittain, come over here. I think this will do."

But my eyes were never still. And before I knew it, I was shouting again, "I don't know, there's another one. Let's look at it first before we cut that one."

Finally, they were both tired of searching, and they made the decision for me.

Pa harvested it, and together they pulled it home. If it was too large for them to handle on their own, Pa went home, harnessed our mule, Toni, hooked him to the sled, and went back to the woods for the tree.

Once home, Pa nailed an **X** made of boards to the trunk bottom so the tree would stand—with a little help from a piece of rope wrapped around the trunk and attached to the wall with staples. It took up a full quarter of the room, sticking out so close to the fireplace, God only knows why everything did not go up in flames.

After that, I bugged Ma Pearl incessantly. I wanted to decorate the tree as soon as it was standing in our living room, but I had to be patient.

"As soon as we finish supper, I'll make the snow," Ma Pearl said. "You know the snow will have to dry overnight. We'll decorate it tomorrow morning."

After supper, she emptied a box of Ivory Snow soap flakes into a dishpan that was half filled with water. She beat it with a hand-operated eggbeater until the soap felt and looked like beaten egg whites. Then, we dipped out handfuls and slathered it onto the tree limbs. The desired effect—fallen snow piled up on the tree branches—was beautiful.

The room—never completely warm—smelled of cedar, Ivory soap, and wood smoke from the fireplace. It was a unique scent that I'll always remember as our own special Christmas incense.

Immediately after breakfast the next morning, we started decorating. I covered the tree with every piece of tinsel we owned. We never had enough decorations to cover the entire tree, but it was beautiful to us.

Since Ma Pearl loved gumdrop trees, each year Pa also presented her with a trimmed—nonpoisonous—thorn bush, which he'd anchored in a can filled with dirt. When she was finished decorating it with gumdrops, it was pretty, and it gave Pa and me something to nibble on throughout the holidays.

At our local store, Fletcher's, hard candies of brilliant colors and shapes, along with striped ribbon candy, stocked the shelves. Sacks of chocolate-drops, with white vanilla centers tasting so rich it made me shiver, fought for space. Ma Pearl's favorite— king-size peppermint logs—were stacked on tabletops.

Our Christmas Eve tradition started when dusk came creeping. It was then that Pa would build a big fire at our woodpile so we could shoot fireworks. After the fireworks, we huddled inside the living room, around the fireplace, and Ma Pearl brought out a big box prepared for just this occasion. It was filled with nuts, oranges, apples, bananas, candy, a coconut, and all the Christmas specialties for a delectable chow down. After gorging ourselves, we went to bed to await Santa.

I slept with Ma Pearl. Every few minutes, I'd whisper, "Reckon he's come yet?"

"No, not yet." She'd whisper back. "Go to sleep or he won't come at all."

One night, I awoke when she was returning to bed. I was instantly alert. "Ma Pearl," I asked, "has he come yet? Please, let's look."

"Well, okay," she said. "I'll turn the light on."

Sure enough, he had been there. Wow! *How in the world did he get down our chimney and over the still glowing coals with all the presents and not get burned?*

Then I begged and begged to open my presents, and Ma Peal gave in and let me open one, before shooing me back to bed.

Instinctively, I always knew which present held my doll.

It was so tough putting her back in her box and crawling back into bed. After Ma Pearl shut the lights off again, I'd lie there quietly, thinking of all the other presents under the tree, and wondering what they were. Most of them, Santa picked up at Fletcher's.

One Christmas, Pa bought Ma Pearl a pretty red flannel gown for Christmas. The first washday after Christmas, all of the wives in the community had a red flannel gown flapping on her clothesline. Fletcher's store had received a shipment of the gowns before Christmas, and all the husbands apparently had the same idea. At the time, we all laughed in glee, but today, I would give anything to see those red flannel gowns flapping in the breeze, or feel Ma Pearl crawling back into bed after having played Santa Claus.

Not even today's Christmas trees, with enough decorations to hide their fakeness, and enough lights to blind the moon, could ever shine as brilliantly as the Christmases of my youth.

The Giving Year

by Julie Bonn Heath

Goose bumps rise on my arms when I remember the Christmas that truly made an impact on my life. It was the Christmas when no presents rested under the tree, yet I received one of the best gifts of all.

I don't remember if we needed an angel to come to us that year because of the bad economy; my parents sheltered us from hearing those things. I know that my dad worked that year on Thanksgiving and Christmas to earn extra money, as he did every year when I was a child, and Mom worked part-time whenever she could.

I wonder if the reason we needed an angel was because we had large bills to pay that year. Although we were only middle class, our house was pretty big. Even though we gathered wood during the winter and burned it in the wood stove, it still must have cost an arm and a leg every month to heat it. As a child, I thought we gathered wood just to make the house cozy, and as a backup for making popcorn and hot cocoa when the electricity went out. I know better, now.

I don't know if the reason we needed a miracle that Christmas was because we had overspent or underbudgeted or if we were just not making it with three kids and related expenses.

What I do know is that when Dad informed us that there would be no gifts that Christmas, both of my brothers and I were upset, and I'm ashamed of that now.

After Dad's announcement, we children lapsed into silence. As they reminded us what Christmas was all about, they remarked that we had taken the news rather well. It was a letdown, just the same. We halfheartedly talked about making each other presents, but that night as I knelt beside my bed, I prayed that somehow we would have a few store-bought toys. And, unable to stop them, big alligator tears rolled down my face.

The next evening it snowed. I looked longingly out of the window at the beautiful drifts and wished that the season were over. Our Christmas tree was bright and pretty, but the lack of presents underneath it depressed me. The holiday felt incomplete.

When the phone rang, I wandered over to tuck myself under Dad's arm and heard him say in surprise, "You're kidding! From who?" I couldn't hear the other end of the conversation, but I do remember that the call was very short.

Dad hung up the phone with a smile on his face. Then, looking at me, he shrugged. "Someone left a card for us at the gas station up the street."

At the gas station, I watched Dad walk back toward the car with an envelope in his hand. I strained to see the mysterious card. *Why would someone drop off a card instead of mailing it? And why not just drop it off at our house, only a mile away?* Dad stomped snow off his shoes as he neared our van. As soon as he opened the door and the cold air rushed in, the windows fogged up, adding an even more mysterious slant to the event.

When Dad opened the card, $200 fell out! Nowhere on the Christmas card or the envelope was there a signature.

"Guess we'll have presents, after all." Dad finally said.

"But who is it from?" I asked, my eyes as wide as saucers.

"I have no idea."

To this day, our giver's identity is unknown. I'm sure there were better things that my parents could have spent that money on. I bet there were unpaid bills and groceries to buy. But they didn't spend it on bills. They gave us gifts. Although at the time the gifts were important, they are all lost in my memory. What does remain is the important part of Christmas that implanted itself in my heart—we were privileged to be recipients of an incredibly unselfish act—a miraculous gift that I will never forget.

Over the years, I have kept that particular memory close to my heart. That Christmas, I learned that no matter how little we may have by our own standards, it may be much compared to someone else's standards. And giving—no matter how much or how little—is a joyous act for both the giver and the receiver.

Making the Magic Last

by Barbara Brady

After the excitement of Christmas Day, some children may think dismantling the Christmas tree is a depressing chore. But in the early 1940s, that was never an issue at our house. As soon as our Christmas Day celebration was over, we immediately stripped the tree. Once the tree was bare, we prepared for a trek back to our grade school.

Mom stood at the door to make certain we wore the sweaters, socks, and mittens she'd knitted for us. She also insisted that we wear those bulky, woolen snow pants that we all hated so much. Bundled until we could barely waddle, we headed for the school, lugging the tree behind us.

Since we lived at the outer limits of the school district, we had to drag our tree about two miles. And if you've never experienced it for yourself, believe me when I say that with the frosty wind blowing off Lake Michigan in Des Plaines, Illinois, two miles can seem like ten. We didn't care. We quickly dragged our tree down the snowpacked, bumpy street, leaving behind a wide and generous evergreen needle trail that would have made Hansel and Gretel envious.

We were in a hurry. Due to the help of our town's firemen, something magical had occurred at the school, and we wanted to be a part of that magic. Every winter the firemen cleared the snow from the school playing field, scooping big piles of snow around the edge of the playground, making a fluffy white rim resembling sherbet. With huge fire hoses hooked to the water hydrants, they flooded the baseball field with torrents of water and transformed it into a shiny lake of ice. Like magic, we had a marvelous ice-skating rink!

We could barely wait to plunge our tree into the snow banks surrounding the ice rink. Our tree would not be the only tree that edged the rink, either. Used Christmas trees appeared from the farthest corners of town. Soon, the frozen pond was surrounded by the heavenly scent of evergreen. In addition to the beauty, the fence of trees sheltered the skaters from the bitter winter wind. Fragments of tinsel, still dangling from the branches of each individual tree, made the barrier glisten in the sunlight.

It was a breathtaking scene.

As with many other families, my sister and I shared a pair of secondhand ice skates. They were huge and probably meant for a man, but we fixed the problem by stuffing wads of socks into the toes. Since Betty Lou was the eldest, she skated first. After several circles around the rink, she glided to the edge of the pond and took off the skates so I could take my turn. Together, we joined the other kids, young and old, with their rosy faces and happy smiles.

More magic came in the form of an old Victrola. One of the neighbors, who lived near the school, put a record player out on his back porch and cranked up the volume. We skated to the thrilling voices of Frank Sinatra, Gene Autry, and Roy Rogers singing Christmas carols.

Our ice-covered field and recycled trees made the holiday season stretch until the ice melted. We marveled at the beauty surrounding us as we whirled, twirled, wobbled, and stumbled. Our community icerink provided hours of exhilarating entertainment for a bunch of kids with few luxuries. No, it wasn't Rockefeller Center. To us, it was much, much better.

I Married Santa Claus

by M. DeLoris Henscheid

𝒥n 1897, a little girl named Virginia O'Hanlon wrote to the *New York Sun* and asked the now-famous question: "Is there really a Santa Claus?" The answer of course: "Yes, Virginia, there really is a Santa Claus." I would like to reaffirm that answer because I have been married to him, for fifty-five years now!

It was in December 1948, when a group of high school kids and young singles, from St. Bernard's Parish in Blackfoot, Idaho, met at the home of Henry and Mary Henscheid for a Christmas party.

I had been out there many times with my friends, Mary and Rosie, but that year something was different. Their older brother, Bernard, who had just returned from the Navy and was currently attending Idaho State College, was home for the holidays.

"Ho-ho-ho," resounded Santa, who vaguely resembled the brother, in spite of the white beard and faded red flannel suit.

After the usual greetings, this Santa did an unusual thing. He went to the piano and began playing Christmas tunes while the group sang their hearts out. His assurance and enthusiasm enticed me to sit next to him on the piano bench.

When the singing ended, he turned and invited each of us to tell him what we wanted for Christmas. When it was my turn, I flirtatiously sat on his lap and claimed I wanted a date. "Well, how about New Year's Eve?" he asked.

It was truly a magical moment for a sixteen-year-old girl! And it has been that same enchantment, which has carried us through the ups and downs of fifty-five years of marriage and nine children.

As a typical Santa, he makes his appearance to the throng of children the Saturday after every Thanksgiving. But this Santa, dressed in a cranberry-red velvet suit, which I made for him, has entered our hometown in many different ways over the years. There have been flashy entrances in fire trucks, wagons pulled by draft horses, a convertible, a police car, a helicopter, and even an army tank. And Bernard has taken his job to heart. He does not just play Santa, he becomes Santa!

Since the very first time he donned the red suit, he has felt it was his calling to respectfully represent the bearer of the Christmas message. Whether reading children's letters on his popular daily radio program, talking with an older child by phone on request of a harried parent, or entering a crowded party, there has always been a reminder that Christmas is the time for helping and giving, not just getting.

And every year, without fail, the children have gifted us with a special moment to cherish. One time, while Bernard was the town Santa, which supplied the much-needed cash for his own family, a dad approached him and asked if he would come out to his vehicle to visit his sons.

Santa crawled into the back of the man's van and sat with four brothers—all wheelchair-bound due to muscular dystrophy. That evening, sitting at the dinner table with his own nine healthy children, he wept with thankfulness.

Annually, hundreds of children greet this familiar Santa with anticipation and excitement when he enters the same homes, crowded school gyms, and churches he has visited for decades with his exuberant bell ringing. Then, handing the bells to a small child, he would turn to the piano, energetically strike the chords and invite everyone to sing.

The crowd joyfully revs up with "Jingle Bells," "Rudolph," Up on the House Top" . . . At the peak of the excitement, he always stops and asks, "Who knows what happens, besides my coming to your house, on Christmas?"

When the crowd proclaims, "It's Baby Jesus' Birthday!" Santa asks everyone to sing "Silent Night."

When the last refrain fades, he would pause for a moment with stilled hands on the keys, his whiskered face bowed.

The profound silence says it all. At that magical moment each year, while watching and waiting in the shadows of the room, this Mrs. Santa felt the same enchantment as that sixteen-year-old girl had so many years ago.

This past year, for the first time in sixty years, my Santa could not make his rounds. It was a sad day for him when he called each name on his long list and repeated, "I guess Santa just went down too many chimneys." As he sat home, missing everyone, the children of Blackfoot gave Santa another unexpected Christmas memory to cherish. Santa had found a permanent place in their hearts. They had not forgotten him.

He received get-well letters, boxes of cookies, cards, visits, and numerous telephone calls from exuberant children explaining they missed the *real* Santa and wished him a speedy recovery. The little ones made it very clear that they were looking forward to the upcoming year when *their* Santa would once again join them in ringing in the best holiday of them all.

The Costume

by Lynn R. Hartz

*a*s Christmas approaches, my mind travels to the Christmases of my past. When I was young, the grade school I attended had six grades and six classrooms. The first four grades always performed a Christmas pageant for the Parent Teacher Association during the month of December.

The year that I was in the second grade, our class presented a play about how the pine tree was chosen to be the beloved Christmas tree. Several children were chosen to be different trees—elm, maple, beech—and I was chosen to be the pine tree, which was interesting because I was the smallest child in the class.

It was an honor to be the Christmas tree, but my part in the play put a little extra burden on my mother, who had to make my costume. She thought and thought about how to make a costume that would resemble a pine tree *and* be something I could wear. Finally, she decided to make my costume out of green crepe paper, which was very heavy material back then.

At the time, Mother had looked at me and then at the paper. When she was done cutting she had two zigzag-shaped crepe paper Christmas trees, exactly the size of me. She then sewed the two together, cutting out a hole in the front for my face, and two slits for my arms.

It fit perfectly, but no one could see who I was, and I felt embarrassment heat my cheeks on the night of the play. I knew that I had been chosen because the teacher really liked me, and I was glad that I wasn't an elm tree or a maple tree, because all the other children could be seen in their costumes!

During the play, my role was to stand on the stage for a long time while the person who was choosing the Christmas tree went around to all the other trees and told them why they weren't chosen. Then, he had to come to me and pretend to "cut me down." Together, we walked to his house, and I was decorated.

At the end of the play, I was weighed down not only by the costume, but also by all of the Christmas ornaments the rest of the children taped onto the crepe-paper costume. To make matters worse, I couldn't even sit down like everyone else. Instead, I had to stand there as the center of attention. I remember my flushed face and how the embarrassment seemed to grow and grow.

It's been fifty-five years since I was a crepe-paper Christmas tree and obviously many things have happened to me. One of the saddest was when my mother died. In her house, I found a cardboard box labeled "Lynn's Baby Things." I was moved to tears when I found the box and knew she had left it especially for me. The first thing that I saw when I opened that box was the green, crepe-paper Christmas tree costume! Not a single thread was broken, not a tear anywhere, and the pieces of tape were still there, just waiting for the ornaments to be attached again.

I held it in my arms and let the memories flow over me. I remembered my mother's face as she'd held the crepe paper up to my body, pins sticking out of her mouth as she sewed. I remembered the joy on her face during the program and the cheerful laughter that accompanied her enthusiastic congratulations after the program. I clearly recall how she had praised me for a job well done.

Today's crepe paper would not survive one night as a child's costume, much less stay together for fifty-five years in a cardboard box. But, then, everything changes over the years—even Christmas. The days of my youth had simpler ways, and I will forever be grateful that my mother thought to save for me a cardboard box filled with the simple yet wondrous treasures of our past.

Thank You, Miss Farley

by Guy Carrozzo

In the mid-1940s, I attended the Walnut Street School in McKeesport, Pennsylvania. On my last visit to my hometown, I was surprised to see that the school had been torn down and replaced with a post office. Although the three-story red brick building was gone, the memory of one teacher who taught there will linger in my mind forever.

McKeesport was a mill town, and the school reflected the same type of discipline that was necessary to survive in the mills. The school was a cold drab place where punishment was meted out with a slap to the face for even a minor infraction of the rules. Each time a student in my class received punishment, I trembled, sick to my stomach.

The bitter feelings I had toward education all changed when a new teacher arrived at our school. Her name was Miss Farley, and I was assigned to her class. Miss Farley brought color and love and kindness to a place that had very little warmth or compassion. She was a warm soul, who always had a smile, a hug, and a word of encouragement. She would share her apple or cookie with you after school—even though you were being kept in for doing something wrong or because you hadn't completed your assignment. We used to wait for her at dismissal time just to be able to walk a few blocks down the street by her side. It was an honor to be in her presence.

Before Miss Farley's arrival, the highlight of our day had been the sounding of the dismissal bell. But after Miss Farley had become our teacher, we shuffled our books, cleaned out our desks, and toddled along, hoping she would ask us to stay to clean the chalkboards. If she didn't ask, we volunteered our services—just to be able to stay with her a little longer.

Despite all this, Miss Farley was not a pushover. She could be strict, and she knew how to hand out discipline. But we always felt the punishment was deserved, and we always knew Miss Farley hated that part of her teaching day. It was as much a punishment for her as it was for the student. She even cried one day when she had to paddle a student.

Miss Farley taught with love, respect, and discipline. She understood the importance of teaching, but more important, she understood that teaching with love, and loving her students, was what teaching is all about.

As Christmas approached that year, our class became more and more excited. We had the best teacher, and we wanted to buy her a great Christmas present. We didn't have much spending money in those days, but we each did our best to turn in pop bottles for deposit and collect paper, rags, and glass by the bushel, which we then sold to the junkman to make a dollar or two. And even though the gift we decided on was just a couple of small, crudely wrapped, inexpensive lace handkerchiefs from the dime store, Miss Farley was so happy and made such a fuss over them that we felt as though we had given her a treasure. How proud she made us all feel! That year, in addition to all she had taught us, we also learned the meaning of giving and that feeling has never left me.

A teacher can never know how far into the future his or her effect on students will be felt, nor how far it will travel, but I hope Miss Farley knew that her teachings went far and wide and that they continue on today in her students and in the people whom we have touched. I know Miss Farley would never be able to remember me—just one little boy in one classroom so many years ago—nor perhaps recall the Christmas gift my class purchased for her, but I will never forget her and what she taught me. She inspired me in ways she could never have known, for I grew up to become a teacher and then became a school principal. I placed a sign above my office door, which read: "SEQUOIA SCHOOL: A BASIC SCHOOL WHERE WE TEACH WITH LOVE, RESPECT, AND DISCIPLINE." Under that sign, it said, "IN HONOR OF MISS FARLEY."

# Do You See What I See?

by Josephine Howard, as told to Lesa Cameron

Greenwood, Nebraska

"**A** what?" my husband, Wayne, asked in surprise.

"A television," I repeated.

It was November 1955, we had two sons: seven and three. Life was busy, life was fun, but times were hard. When visiting school one day, my son's teacher took me aside and said, "Mrs. Howard, you know Steve's the only child in kindergarten through second grade classroom without a television, and he's feeling it. He's left out of their games and conversations. He should have one." It took only a quick mental tally of the fifteen children in his room to know she was speaking the truth.

But what could we do? My husband, a rural mail carrier, needed a large portion of our income for parts to keep his car in working condition—seventy-eight miles a day of dirt and gravel roads took their toll. There was no money for a television set.

We had planned that this Christmas would be celebrated with more love than presents. And that had been just fine by us, because we had plenty of love to share. But now, with the idea planted by Steve's teacher, would we, could we, afford a television set for Christmas?

My husband visited the appliance store in the small town next to ours, just to test the waters and see what was out there. As we had suspected, the new sets came too dearly for us to afford. Discouraged, he turned to leave when he spotted a small used set sitting by itself. In a blond wooden cabinet, the thirteen-inch screen looked wonderful, especially when he spied the price of $35. Perhaps we could afford a television, after all. My husband asked the salesman to hold it for a day and then hurried home to discuss it with me.

It would be difficult, but if it was the only present for the entire family, and if the grocery store would give us credit for a week, we could do it. So with anxious hearts, we put $10 down on the black-and-white set, to hold it until Christmas—just three weeks away. Then it would have to be paid for in full.

Christmas preparations went on with stifled excitement. No store-bought tree for us—we preferred the excitement of the hunt and stalked a wild cedar in its natural habitat. After finding the perfect tree—and obtaining permission from the farmer who owned the property—my husband cut it down and hauled it home. I baked Christmas cookies, and with the help of the children, decorated them with sprinkles and frosting. Then, using red and white crepe paper, I wrapped the stairwell poles so they looked like huge, straight sticks of peppermint candy.

Soon the house was scented with cedar, and the delicious sweet smells of holiday baking. Only then did we set up the cardboard "red brick" fireplace next to the tree to signify that Christmas had arrived.

My husband sneaked over to pick up the set a few days before Christmas, then put it in our basement where I hid it beneath a quilt. On Christmas Eve, after the children were in bed, Mr. and Mrs. Claus made their appearance. Each stocking was filled with an orange, a candy cane, and a few mixed nuts. Then a small metal car was carefully wrapped, and one placed in each stocking. Steve had one extra item this year; a printed note directing him to the living room for a treasure hunt.

Christmas morning came early, as it always does in a home with small children. Happy sounds—the emptying of stockings, and cars being driven on the hardwood floor— were interrupted as Steve found the note. Carefully, he read it aloud, and then turned a puzzled face toward me. I urged our other son, Ted, to put down his new car and follow his brother into the living room.

Yelling in excitement, as if turned loose from school for summer vacation, Steve bolted to the living room to look behind the big blue rocking chair as the note had directed. When he spied the huge box shape, covered by a quilt he began to work frantically to move the heavy rocker and pull off the blanket.

Suddenly, the beautiful lights on our Christmas tree were eclipsed by the radiant shining smile on our son's face. For just a moment stunned silence reigned, then excited screams burst out. Child and parent alike stared wide-eyed as television came into our lives.

Today, we have a modern television set—a Christmas gift from our four grown children. But we will always hold dear the memory of a young boy, thrilled beyond words to receive a black-and-white TV so many years ago.

# Spotlight on Greenwood, Nebraska

## Greenwood History

Greenwood was named after hunter/trapper Silas Greenwood, who moved into the area in 1862 and who is considered to have been the first permanent settler. Silas settled east of the current village, along a creek that still bears his name. Another creek that flows past Greenwood was a serious disappointment to the early settlers. In a land where water is precious, it was discouraging to come across a creek that was unusable. The creek, which passes over large salt flats, is aptly named Salt Creek.

## Industry

Agriculture is Greenwood's main industry, past and present. The Farmers Co-operative elevators dominate the skyline. In 1987, Baker's Candies opened and began to make its mark in the chocolate industry nationwide, bringing recognition as well as jobs to Greenwood. One gas station and the newly arrived Yoder's Amish Furniture & More (2003) complete the business profile.

## Transportation

Trains provided public transportation from 1870 until the mid-1900s, and for a brief time in the mid-1900s a bus line serviced Greenwood. Currently, however, automobiles are the only mode of transportation.

## In the Know

In the 1800s, more times than not, poor roads and extreme weather conditions isolated residents. Oftentimes, the town newspaper was the only means of obtaining information. Greenwood residents were exceedingly fortunate when Mr. and Mrs. W. S. Elliott began publishing the *Greenwood Eagle* on October 14, 1881. The *Eagle* was replaced in 1884 by the *Greenwood Hawk-Eye*, which lasted until 1887, when it was replaced by the *Greenwood Leader*. In 1889 the *Greenwood Gazette* began and continued in publication until 1934.

Since 1881, Greenwood newspapers have become a valuable historical link with the day-to-day lives of people living during the early days. Many records, some of which were inconsistent, have sustained damage or were lost due to fires and storms, such as the destructive tornado, which hit Greenwood on Easter Sunday, March 23, 1913.

## Early Politics

The first governing body for Greenwood was appointed by the Cass county clerk to serve until an election could take place more than a year later in November 1884. As a village, Greenwood does not have a mayor. Instead, Greenwood is governed by an elected board of trustees. Each year, the trustees elect one of their own members to serve as chairman.

On November 5, 1916, William Jennings Bryan, three time presidential hopeful, Nebraska congressman, and secretary of state (appointed by President Woodrow Wilson), spoke at the Greenwood Opera House collecting the largest crowd ever assembled there to that date. All available seats in town were carried to the site of his speech, and still many in the crowd were forced to stand. His talk was aimed at "convincing all voters that to vote 'dry' was the only way." Greenwood became a "dry" community through a local vote in the spring of 1917. Two years later, on April 1, 1919, twenty-two courageous women became the first women in the history of the Greenwood precinct to join the male populous in casting their vote against allowing alcohol in the community.

## Fire Takes a Toll

In its early years, Greenwood was plagued by fire. Blazes swept through Greenwood in January 1914, April 1917, and again in January 1924. With no organized fire department and a critical shortage of water, Greenwood residents were forced to rely on the assistance of a town fifteen miles away, and help often arrived too late. In 1924, however, following the third fire, the town of Greenwood rallied and installed a public water system.

## Greenwood Today

With most of the working population commuting 20 to 100 miles round trip per day, Greenwood has become a bedroom community. The town no longer has grocery stores, a school, or a depot, but it has tenaciously held on to its state-accredited library, which helps keep the borders of Greenwood limitless.

The Nebraska state motto truly applies when it comes to this town, because for those who crave small towns, Greenwood is truly "the good life."

## Hollywood Holiday

by Kathy L. Reed

My grandfather was never a good provider, as my grandmother and her four children will attest. During the Depression, when he did stay home long enough to work, jobs were hard to find. He once held a job on a road team for a dollar a week, but most of the time, he worked as a sharecropper for whomever he could get to hire him.

But despite hard times, my grandmother was very disappointed in 1938 when she rattled the old glass jar that held the money she made selling eggs—when she had eggs to sell. That Christmas, there had been no extra eggs, and her savings had dwindled to six cents. There wasn't enough money to buy her children anything for Christmas.

In desperation, she searched every inch of the house—old pocketbooks, coat pockets, Granddaddy's pants pockets, and even under pictures in picture frames, where she had sometimes hidden money to keep my grandfather from spending it for what she always called "some fool thing!"

As she looked at the faces of her children over an oatmeal breakfast the next morning, she couldn't bear to think of how waking up on Christmas to no toys would affect those faces.

Not wanting to give in to the inevitable, she mulled it over in her mind all day and finally came up with a plan.

After my grandfather left for the field the next morning, she put her plan into motion. The first thing she did was give the older children instructions to watch the younger ones, then she patted her worn apron down over her even more worn-out dress, straightened the bobby pins in her hair, and walked down the dirt road toward a little white cottage. Knocking on their neighbor's door with more courage than she felt, Granny waited patiently until the lady of the house came to the door.

When the door opened, my grandmother did what any self-respecting mother would do in a case such as this: she swallowed her pride.

Looking her neighbor in the eye, Granny asked if the woman needed any help with anything—adding that she needed the money for Christmas for her children. The lady of the house was very surprised to be asked. They were a very poor family, too, and money was scarce. But she also realized Granny's need was strong, and since her own children were older, there were some toys lying around her home that were no longer useful. Perhaps she and Granny could reach a mutual understanding after all.

The woman immediately asked Granny inside and showed her two naked baby dolls. Both had been loved, as was evident from their messy hair and chewed fingers and toes. The lady also pointed out two toy trucks. The trucks were a little rusty, but the wheels still rolled. Within minutes, these two proud country women had come up with a plan. Granny would do the neighbor's laundry in return for the old toys.

Each morning, my grandmother got up at dawn, took care of her own chores and then made breakfast. As soon as Granddaddy left for the fields, Granny went to the neighbor's house, dragged out an old cast-iron wash pot, and gathered wood for a fire, cutting pieces of lye soap into the water that she used to clean. Sweat poured into her eyes and at times it felt like her back was going to break in two. But, according to the verbal contract she and her neighbor had agreed on, she continued doing the work of two women for two weeks.

Granny kept her secret, never telling anyone why she was helping the neighbor. Finally, the toys belonged to her.

Pleased that her children would have gifts under their Christmas tree after all, Granny carefully packed the toys away in a box, which she then hid in the pantry. Each night, after she tucked her children into bed and added wood to the fire, she brought out the dolls. She spent hours washing the dolls, brushing and styling their hair, and creating clothing for them from feed sacks and from clothes her children had outgrown.

The trucks got a washing and a coat of blue paint covered the rust. And although Granny could barely read and write, by the time she was finished, each truck bore the name of one of her two sons.

My mother, Lucille—only five years old that Christmas— was one of the little girls. Her sister, Louise, was nine, and her brothers were seven and three. Mom said she and her siblings had expected to get something like apples, and maybe, if they were lucky, some penny candy. But that Christmas, under a wobbly but beautiful small pine tree decorated with gum balls wrapped in shiny foil, they found the two dolls with the hand-made clothes, and the bright blue trucks with clean black tires.

I can't tell you how excited the children must have been that day, but I know it touched my mother deeply. She still gets tears in her eyes whenever she talks about that particular Christmas when her mother worked so hard to make sure her children received what Mom has always called "the most beautiful dolls in the world." Those dolls were made beautiful by the loving hands of a woman who believed the true meaning of Christmas was love and who made sure her children got plenty of it that year.

# A Small Town Christmas Story

by Jeanne Converse

It was December 1955. I stood in the middle of our living room trying to decide where to put the Christmas tree. I never got tired of looking at the newly installed bay window, the shiny hardwood floor, and the rose-colored walls. We had purchased the old house a couple of years before, and slowly, stick-by-stick, it was coming together the way we dreamed it would.

John, my husband, worked long hours at the paper mill and spent all his spare time tearing out walls, ripping up floors, and replacing them with sturdy modern materials. I took care of our two toddlers: three-year-old Anne and two-year-old Mike. Between household jobs, I painted the finished walls and prepared the casings and baseboards for installation. We were happy and proud of our accomplishments. This Christmas, for the first time, our entire family would be celebrating the holiday at our house. I could hardly wait.

On the morning of December 20, we awoke to a very cold house. The outdoor thermometer read twenty below zero and our old pot-bellied wood stove had reduced its contents to ashes. While John was getting ready for work, I stuffed the stove with newspapers, piled on a few logs, and flicked in a match.

John grabbed a cup of coffee and a blueberry muffin on his way out the door. Anne and Mike sat huddled together, wrapped in a blanket, patiently waiting for the hot chocolate I was preparing for them. Sipping on hot chocolate and nibbling on muffins, eventually, we felt the cozy warmth of the stove begin to replace the cold chill in the air.

Lulled by our drowsy warmth, I jolted out of my chair when I heard frantic voices yelling, "Your house is on fire!" Before I could react, someone crashed through the door.

Suddenly, one of our neighbors was at my side, wrapping the children in a blanket and whisking them out to her car while I snatched the phone and called my father. Then I grabbed the drawer with our important papers and raced outside. I dropped my load on the ground and charged back inside, ignoring the danger. With Christmas just five days away I was determined to rescue the suit I had purchased and paid for—one dollar a week for almost a year—for John. It was to be his Christmas present. A stranger grabbed my arm and dragged me out of the house.

Meanwhile, my dad notified the mill, and John returned home. But there was nothing we could do to save our house. In less than an hour, our dream home had been reduced to one lonely chimney among a pile of ashes.

Numb, we moved in with my parents. Almost immediately, the phone and doorbell began to ring. Everyone, friends and strangers alike, wanted to help. The donated clothes in Mom's spare bedroom would eventually replenish the Red Cross inventory. My friends from Home Bureau replaced my canned goods from their own shelves. The milkman donated extra milk and eggnog. The neighborhood grocer delivered a turkey and all the trimmings. We also received many wrapped Christmas gifts, as well as anonymous envelopes with ten or twenty-dollar bills in them.

As we sat in the church during Christmas mass, I thought about the happenings of the last few days. This had been the most devastating Christmas any of us had ever experienced. All our dreams had indeed gone up in smoke, but somehow I felt extremely blessed. The outpouring from our community was something that will remain with me and my family forever. As I sat there, humbled by the love that surrounded us, I bowed my head and said a sincere prayer of thanks for I knew we would—and best of all, we could—start over again.

Grandma's Gift

by Michelle Mach

"**Y**ou just don't understand!"

The latest argument with my mom echoed in my brain as I grabbed handfuls of new hardbacks and arranged them in the bargain bin at the bookstore where I worked. It was late October and already the rush for Christmas was in full swing. A recent college graduate, I was living at home and trying to figure out what to do with my life. Mom seemed reluctant to let me go, and I was eager to grow up and move away.

For Christmas a few years earlier, Mom had surprised me by repairing two of my favorite dolls from my toddler years. Molly, a cloth doll with black, fuzzy hair, cross-stitch eyes and pink cheeks—courtesy of some lipstick snatched from Mom's purse, and Leslie, who boasted orange yarn hair, a navy vinyl dress, and a tinny, but commanding voice: *"My name is Les-lie. Tie my shoes! Snap my jacket!"*

Even at the age of two, my impatience at growing up was already evident; the photo album overflows with snapshots of me pushing my dolls in the stroller, feeding them in a high-chair, and even potty-training them.

I was in my late teens the Christmas that Mom surprised me with the dolls. I tried to be grateful, but inside I was totally over it.

I grabbed another stack of children's books to place in the bargain bin and stopped dead in my tracks. There before me was a pale, peachy-pink book with the words *Miss Flora* plastered across the front. I picked up the small, square book and held it in my hand, remembering a story I'd heard once before in my early teens.

It was 1947 in Lupton, Michigan, and my mother was five years old. A middle child—between two sisters and an older brother—Mom had light curly hair, an inquisitive expression, and new glasses. That Christmas, she poured over the Sears & Roebuck Co. catalog, dreaming of possibilities, particularly the dolls—dolls with frilly dresses, dolls with cascades of blonde curls, dolls with eyes that opened and shut. While the snow fell outside, my mother sat at the kitchen table in the farmhouse and dreamed.

But there was no doll under the Christmas tree that year. Instead, she received a small hardbound book, *Miss Flora McFlimsey's Christmas Eve* by Mariana. That fall, Mom had begun the quarter-mile walk down the gravel road with her siblings to the Withey School. As much as she loved school, there were no books for young readers there or in her home. Mom had hugged the book to her chest and studied the bright watercolor illustrations. Not only was this her first book, but it was the first gift that belonged completely to her alone.

In the following days, in between games of Flinch and feeding the chickens, she pretended that she was the girl in the story with the beautiful doll who magically appeared under the Christmas tree.

I smiled as I set the book aside. The little girl who had clung to Miss Flora grew up to be a mother who helped me struggle through my first chapter book and later created a private reading corner in my bedroom using two bookcases and a big floor pillow. The same mother who had cried with me when, as a lonely eighth-grader, I was forced to give away many books that would not fit into the moving van.

I suddenly realized that though Mom and I do not always agree, we are connected in so many important ways. Glancing at the book again, I realized with a start that our connection went even deeper than even I recognized. Though I had never really known my grandmother—she had lived more than 2,500 miles away and had died when I was only eleven—we also were connected. When Grandma gave *Miss Flora* to my mother—all those years ago—she had also passed on the gift of a lifetime to me.

The Best Party Ever

by Phyllis Nagle

$\mathcal{A}$s we stood stiffly at the Sullivan's door, I eyed my husband, Jon. He wore his only suit, a starched white shirt, and a blue tie with white pin drops that reminded me of snowflakes. I had a pricey new haircut and was wearing my green princess-style taffeta dress, patent leather shoes, and a purse to match. While we waited to be welcomed in, I envisioned a cozy living room complete with a huge Christmas tree illuminated by yellow lights, decorated with old-fashioned ornaments and a brilliant silver star. I imagined flickering candles, a long winding staircase with garlands of fresh evergreens accented with holly boughs, and a kitchen offering up aromas of roasted turkey and hot apple cider.

When we had driven in the driveway a few minutes ago, we had hesitated. There weren't any other cars in the drive, and we hadn't wanted to be the first guests. But we decided to be brave and ring the bell, anyway.

Nervously, I glanced at my dress. I had spent the early part of the day preparing for this party. I wasn't sure about the dress code for an invitation to a "Christmas Open House," and I hoped I was not underdressed. The Sullivan's were a well-established, traditional couple who had recently moved from a small town on the East Coast. I hadn't met them yet, and though Jon and Bob had attended the same high school, he hadn't met Bob's wife yet either. When they ran into each other in town, Bob had invited Jon and me to his upcoming Christmas party. A formal invitation followed.

As I stood on the Sullivan's doorstep reliving the sequence that had led to this invitation, Mrs. Sullivan opened the door. After an awkward moment, the front door closed firmly and Jon and I turned around and walked back to our car. In silence, we climbed into our old Chevy sedan and shut the doors. For a moment, we sat quietly together in the dark.

I shuddered. "How embarrassing!" I turned and looked at my husband in the dim light. *The party wasn't until next weekend! How could I have gotten the date wrong?* "It's my fault," I said.

Jon shook his head. "We both goofed," he said reassuringly.

I glanced back at the house. "Don't you think she could've been nicer?"

Jon loosened his tie and started the engine. "I think we shocked her."

As we drove away, I gazed longingly at the house. Though the grey skies and drizzle of the evening was typical weather for December, the ribbon of smoke rising from the chimney made me think of how warm and inviting it must be inside of their home.

In frustration, I looked down at my new dress. I couldn't decide whether to cry or throw something. I had wasted good money buying a new dress and hiring a babysitter for our young son, which was an extravagance. We had never hired a sitter before.

As the windshield wipers clapped back and forth in front of my face, I recalled the awkward scene that had taken place just moments before. How silly I must have appeared to Mrs. Sullivan.

"Where do we go now?" I asked. My disappointment was evident. It wasn't often we received an invitation out, and I had been looking forward to the evening.

"Home?" Jon said.

"No, let's stop by Dave and Carol's," I said, hoping our closest friends would be home. I didn't want the evening to end on a disappointing note. Jon agreed, so we drove across town to our friends' condominium.

"I'll wait in the car," he said. "Signal if they're open to our invasion."

I flew up the steps. Carol opened the door and a delicious scent of cinnamon swirled past her red apron and enveloped me. I breathed deeply and sighed.

Her face lit up and she smiled brightly. "What's up?" She asked.

I shook my head. "We blew it."

Within minutes, Jon and I had been welcomed inside and were sitting in front of their fireplace. And though Dave was swamped with paperwork, he rose and greeted us with a warm smile.

"Take off your tie, Jon," he said with a laugh. "I don't recognize you!"

"It's not so funny," I declared. "We've had their fancy invitation for weeks—stationery from Gumps, no less!"

"Invitation—from whom?" Carol asked as she returned from the kitchen carrying a tray with four glasses filled with eggnog.

Jon raised his eyebrows, "The Sullivan's—Bob Sullivan. We grew up together. His parents and mine are still close friends."

Jon and I exchanged a glance. We both were worried that Jon's parents would hear about our lack of social polish.

Jon shook his head. "You should have seen Bob's wife's face. She was dressed in jeans and a college sweatshirt, wearing no makeup. We stood there in clothes looking as out of place as trick-or-treaters at a Fourth of July picnic. I'll never forget her horrified look."

216    Classic Christmas

Suddenly, it all seemed funny. Soon we were all laughing, and I was comfortable again. That was when I realized that the true meaning of Christmas is being with good friends. With real friends, I could be myself and laugh at my own flaws.

On the way home that evening, Jon took my hand in his. "Did the evening turn out okay for you?"

I smiled. "It turned out to be the best Christmas party—my favorite date and two of our best friends. I'm glad I went."

## Miracle on Rolling Acres Drive

by Debbie Hill

*A* month before Christmas, I searched the *Farmer's Almanac* for the long-range weather forecast. I'd always yearned for a white Christmas—the kind I'd seen in the movies and on Christmas cards, and I hoped this would be the year. It was all I could do to keep my enthusiasm contained when I read the *Almanac*'s prediction—a hard winter for South Texas.

My family laughed at the idea, telling me to dream on. They suggested I take a trip to Maine if I wanted snow. Moving was out of the question, so I prayed.

A couple of days before Christmas, the weather forecast in the local newspaper included the possibility of snow. I circled the article and smugly waved it in my son's face. As I prepared dinner on Christmas Eve, I looked out the window every few minutes. My fear was that it would actually snow, but that it would melt as soon as it hit the ground, and I would miss it. But God works in mysterious ways, and my prayers were answered that evening when the phone rang.

On the other end, my daughter, D'wann shouted, "Mom, it's snowing!" Her voice was like that of an awestruck child.

I ran to the front door, and there it was—sleet.

Disappointed, I watched for a while and then returned to the kitchen. Five minutes later, I opened the front door and checked again. There was a difference in the air. A thin white layer covered the ground and the porch banister. On closer inspection, I realized the cold white layer was too fluffy for sleet. I looked toward the streetlights and saw particles swirling and dancing in the glow. Snow! I ran back inside and yelled for my son. After turning off the stove, I ran out to stand in the yard and let the snow fall into my hands. I tasted it on my tongue and watched in delight as it accumulated on my shoulders. As I looked up into the swirling whiteness, I thanked God for answering my prayers.

All around me, the neighborhood came to life. My son and grandson frolicked about, attempting to make a snowman and throwing snowballs. Neighbors took to the streets. Adults romped and played, yelling to one another, "Can you believe it?" and "Merry Christmas!"

My son, Ben, who had experienced hard winters in the Ukraine for the past eight years, quickly showed the neighbors how to raise their windshield wipers to prevent their motors from freezing. That lesson was just the first of many we sunflowers from South Texas were to learn. We also found out that snow will clean your tennis shoes to perfection, and insulate and protect your plants, and that in order to make a snowman you need packy snow. Now I know how someone from the North feels when they come to our beaches and try to build their first sandcastle!

After a lot of fun and the realization I sorely needed a scarf, hat, and a heavier coat, I stepped inside to answer the ringing phone. My other daughter, Stefnie, had just walked out of the movie theater and into a winter wonderland. The disbelief and wonder in her voice was priceless. After we hung up, I realized that by now the snow was probably reaching the east side of town. I dialed my cousin and told her to look outside and see if it was snowing. Her doubt turned to sheer delight when she and her family realized what was happening.

That night, I set the alarm for 5:00 A.M.. As soon as I awoke, I had an urge to look outside. I resisted. I was so afraid the snow would be melted. I reminded myself that just hoping and waiting for a miracle is a gift in itself and that the dream in my soul wasn't as important as the soul in my dream. Finally, I opened the curtains and peered outside. It was as if I had just pulled the ribbon off a huge gift from God. Other than the second that a newborn enters the world, the sight outside my window had to be the most beautiful sight I have ever seen. My wish had come true. Everything was blanketed in eight inches of snow!

The Giving Season

by John R. Gugel

There is a bite to the air tonight, a sign in this area of Wisconsin that Christmas is not far off. Soon it will be time again to set out our manger scene on the front porch. It will stay there until the first warm day in the New Year when the figurines, having frozen solidly to the porch, thaw loose. Then, we wrap them in newspaper and put them away until the next Christmas holiday rolls around.

The figures, the tallest of which stands eleven inches high, are ceramic. The stable was built out of rough textured wood, probably old barn boards. The figures are fragile and over the past fourteen Christmases, several figures have been broken beyond repair. We have only one camel left but that is fine since we are down to one wise man. One of the shepherds stands in for Joseph, an early casualty. Baby Jesus has lost one hand.

We continue to put the set out on the front porch not just because it is Christmas, but also as a reminder of the kindness of strangers. You see, we came into possession of this fine set in a wonderful way.

We had lived in Muskego only four months when it came time to celebrate Christmas. We had always lived in cities, and it was an adjustment to sit at the kitchen table and see the neighbor's cows just outside the window. We felt somewhat lonely and more than a little lost that first Christmas. We had not realized how much we would miss our friends in Iowa.

One evening, I looked outside and saw a stranger rushing from our garage toward his pick-up, which was parked in our driveway. I went to the door and called out, "Do you need something?"

"No, we just wanted to welcome you to town," the man answered as he jumped into his truck, backed out onto the road, and sped off into the night.

I glanced toward the garage and saw three boxes sitting in front of the door. When we opened them, we found the wooden stable and all the figures, intact but somewhat worn. We found out later that the stranger's name was Bob and that he was known all over town for his thoughtfulness. His good deeds, always done anonymously, were legendary in this town where no one is really anonymous.

At first, we put the set under our Christmas tree in the living room, but that seemed selfish. So, instead, we put it outside on the front porch and that is where it sits every year. Granted, it puts the figures at some risk, but we want others to enjoy it. Mostly, we leave it there as one small way of passing on to others the kindness shown to us by a stranger fourteen years ago.

The Perfect Gift

by Dianne Neal Matthews
Ripley, Tennessee

*I* was enjoying first grade to the fullest, until one day in December when the little girl behind me set the tiniest Christmas present imaginable on her desk. It was less than one inch on each side, wrapped with white glossy paper, and tied up with a sliver of red cellophane. I was captivated. I had never seen anything so exquisite. Day after day the tiny gift caught my eye, and my active imagination tried to guess what miniature treasure might be inside. It had to be something wondrous beyond description.

I longed for that object with all the power a five-year old can muster. Finally, I became convinced that it should be mine. I deserved it because I desired it. Since I rode an early bus to school, it was a simple matter to slip into the empty classroom one morning. My hands eagerly tore open the tiny present. Inside, I found nothing.

Staring at the destruction in my hand, anticipation dissolved into disappointment and confusion. Gradually, my stunned mind grasped the fact that the little package had been nothing more than a hollow decoration. I sat at my desk with the torn paper and an empty feeling growing inside of me. I was sickened by the knowledge of my guilt.

It was a scene that would repeat itself many times in my life.

As I grew up, the world enticed me with all sorts of shiny, gaily wrapped "presents" that caught my eye and promised happiness. Too often, when I accepted what the world was offering and tore away the wrappings, my excitement was replaced by feelings of emptiness. Over and over, I found myself proving the old cliché: You can't judge a gift by its wrapping.

One Christmas, as I carefully arranged the pieces of our nativity scene, I was struck by the humble setting of the event that lies at the heart of the season: an insignificant village, an obscure young couple, a rustic stable, shepherds and animals, and a baby lying in a manger. *Who would have picked such a lowly setting for the most precious gift ever given?*

Today, I still struggle with the tendency to be deceived by the outward appearance of a gift. As Christmas draws near, it's especially easy for me to be attracted to the fancy wrappings of what the world offers and to unwittingly long for packages that are empty inside. I may take my eyes off the gifts that truly matter, like listening to the soft strains of "Silent Night," seeing the wonders of the season reflected in the shining eyes of a child, or even in the simple act of choosing just the right gift for someone I love or for an anonymous child in need of help. If I'm not careful, I may even shift my focus off the gift whose grace is the reason we celebrate.

So every December, I remember that long-ago morning when I stole a Christmas present. And every December—all over again—I am grateful that God gives his gifts freely. He never disappoints me.

# Spotlight on Ripley, Tennessee

## Town Facts

**Population:** 7,844
**Incorporated:** 1838
**Location:** Ripley is located 52 miles north
of Memphis, 185 miles west of Nashville, and
16 miles east of the Mississippi River.

## The History of Ripley

The main occupation of the early settlers was clearing the wilderness with their bare hands to cultivate the land and plant crops. The area was once part of the hunting grounds of the Chickasaw Indians, who were friendly to the English-speaking settlers.

In 1901, when the town of Ripley was rechartered—unbeknownst to the town's forefathers—a twist of humor was incorporated into the wording. The new charter contains a line that has on occasion attracted national attention—one boundary is described as running "thence north 85 degrees, east to a black gum marked with a cross and with mistletoe on the top, and with a blue bird sitting on a limb."

## Industry

Because of the many acres of centuries-old forests along the Mississippi River, lumber has always been a major product in this area of Tennessee. In the early 1900s, several lumber mills, logging companies, and stave saw mills operated in the county.

A number of large industrial businesses have operated in Ripley, also, but throughout history, Ripley has been mainly dependent on agriculture. Cotton is still the largest crop, though truck crops such as apples, peaches, soybeans, and strawberries, are also important. From spring through fall, highways are dotted with local farmers selling their produce from stands or truck beds.

The Ripley Box and Basket Company was founded in 1921 and produced fruit and vegetable crates and bushel baskets, which were shipped all over the United States in addition to being sold to local farmers. The factory burned down in the early 1970s.

Business today include Marvin Windows and Doors, American Greetings Corporation, Siegel-Robert Automotive Ripley South, Siegel-Robert Automotive Ripley North (custom electroplating), and Komatsu America Corporation (parts distribution for mining and construction equipment).

## The Naming of a Town

As more communities developed in west Tennessee, new counties were organized from portions of larger, existing counties. On November 24, 1835, a new bill was passed to establish Lauderdale County out of parts of Haywood, Dyer, and Tipton counties. Then in 1836, county commissioners were appointed to select a site for the county seat, which was to be named after General Eleazer Ripley, who was a hero in the War of 1812.

## Places of Note

Ripley's newest public park includes four multipurpose athletic fields, a walking/jogging trail, sand volleyball, horseshoes, four tennis courts, several pavilions, and a swimming pool featuring a 332-foot water slide.

Lauderdale Cellars is a family-owned and -operated business with the largest vineyard in west Tennessee. The winery produces a variety of fine wines and offers tours and complimentary samples as well as The Wine Rack, a gift shop that stocks antiques, art, silver, crystal, jewelry, and more.

The current Lauderdale County courthouse (the fourth one) was built in 1936 and was listed on the National Register of Historic Places on March 30, 1995.

## Ripley Tomatoes

Ripley is known as the home of the "Ripley tomato," which is popular throughout the eastern United States. Agricultural experts say that the acidity in the county's soil makes the area close to the Mississippi River especially good for growing tomatoes. (In 2004, Tennessee voted the tomato the official state fruit.) Fifty county farmers grow a wide variety of tomatoes on approximately 1,200 acres of fertile soil. In 1983, in honor of the Ripley tomato, the city established the Lauderdale County Tomato Festival, an annual three-day celebration held in July. Activities include tomato recipe tasting, a tomato contest (biggest, smallest, best taste, best color, oddest, and ugliest), a 5K run, a carnival, a barbecue cook-off, a beauty contest, live entertainment, and more.

## Ripley's Walk of Fame

Singer Tina Turner was born and raised in a nearby community and at one time worked in Ripley. In January 1993, Tina donated $50,000 to establish the Tina Turner Child Abuse Center in Ripley.

The Gift of a Brother

by Barbara Anton

Our little Pennsylvania mountain town lay under a pall on Christmas in 1935. One of the town's most beloved ladies had been killed in an auto accident a few days before, leaving behind a husband and five children. Though the women of Pocono Pines had rallied, Christmas would be bleak for the Franks family.

I accompanied Mother when she delivered her potato casserole. There were no gifts under their tree. I wasn't surprised, but when I looked at the children's faces, I felt their disappointment. I knew that the Great Depression had left Mr. Franks out of work. There would be no gifts under many trees that year. As an only child, Santa had granted both my requests, and I had joyfully torn open the wrappings on a beautiful doll and a much wanted checkerboard. Now, standing in the Frank's sparsely furnished home, I realized how lucky I was.

When we returned home that day, I looked at my gifts through different eyes. I couldn't get the image of the lonely tree in the Franks's home out of my mind. I picked up my doll and cuddled her while I contemplated the checkerboard. Dad and I had eagerly awaited Santa's visit so we could play checkers together. I thought of Roy Franks, who was in my grade, and his father. *How sad they must be.* I couldn't help but wonder if playing checkers together with his father would make Roy forget the loss of his mother for even a moment.

"Mother," I asked, "Do you think Santa would mind if I shared my gifts with Roy?"

She looked up questioningly, probably remembering the sacrifices she and Dad had made to buy those gifts. "But Santa brought just what you asked for. Don't you like your gifts?"

"Oh, yes, I do," I answered quickly. "But Roy didn't get anything. Can't I give him my checkerboard?"

"I thought you wanted to play checkers with me," Dad said from behind his newspaper.

"Well, yes, I did—I do. But Roy looked so sad. I thought maybe he'd like to play checkers with his dad."

Dad put the newspaper down then and looked at me. "I guess Santa won't mind if you share."

Mother helped me re-wrap the checkerboard, and Dad drove us to their house. Roy answered our knock, and when I handed the gift to him, he dropped his eyes and shifted uneasily. "Thanks," he muttered.

At first, we avoided each other during third-grade recess; each embarrassed by the exchange. But a few days later, when the school bully attempted to steal my milk money, Roy came to my defense. It was to become a pattern throughout our lives.

As children, we played together, and when the Franks moved into the house next door, Roy helped me with my chores. He took the shovel from my hands and mucked out the chicken coop; then he spread the manure on Mother's flowerbed, as I had been instructed to do. He helped me wash the car, and he pitched in when I had to weed the garden. As children, we developed a camaraderie akin to that of brother and sister. As teenagers, we double-dated, and we've remained friends throughout our lives.

I gave the gift of an insignificant checkerboard, and in exchange was given one of the most precious gifts life has to offer: a devoted, caring brother. At least that's what I perceive Roy Franks to be.

The Dog Saved the Day

by Marcia E. Brown

Ozark Mountain lore is rich with dog stories.

In my childhood days at Fort Smith, Arkansas, most families had tales of their Old Blues, Old Yellers, and Sheps. Most everyone has at least one story of a beloved canine that was, in their eyes, almost human.

In our family, that special dog was Chandu—named after my favorite radio character. From puppyhood, Chandu was exceptional. Part collie, part sheepdog, his thick black fur was set off by a white ruff around his neck and front, and at the tip of his plumed tail. And, according to my dad, his widely spaced eyes were a sign of intelligence.

From the first day of mutual adoption, Chandu seemed to know exactly what was expected of him and was easy to train. In short order, Dad taught him to sit, stay, come, and lie down. Chandu acquiesced to use the leash, but he would nudge it and give us a look that said clearly, *All right, if you must, but you know I don't need it.* And he did not, for he quickly learned to heel and to follow closely behind his human companion's left side.

Chandu loved riding in the car and having a long run in the country. He went with us on all our outings into the mountains.

It was in December during the early days of World War II that Chandu saved us from a miserable, if not worse, Christmas. On Christmas Eve 1942, Dad found time and enough rationed gas to take us into the hills north of town to collect cedar branches for holiday decorating.

Chandu ran back and forth while Dad and Mom cut evergreen boughs and holly, thick with berries, and loaded it into our old Studebaker. The winter sun was bright when Dad built a fire on the rocks near the creek so we could roast hot dogs and marshmallows. Afterward, Dad led the way up the heavily wooded hillside, where we climbed to a high ridge for a fine view of the mountains. Chandu ran freely, following one of us, then another.

Time passed and clouds suddenly sprang from the west, bringing December twilight early on this happy afternoon. We started the long descent back toward the road where Dad had parked the car. In the quickly growing dimness and dense woods, Dad lost his way, which made us all uneasy. Wild hogs roamed the thick brush and forest. In the winter, they could be more dangerous to hikers than rattlesnakes. Rustlings in the dense undergrowth made us nervous, especially when Chandu growled in response.

Dad remembered we had climbed over a fence high on the hillside, yet when we stumbled into one, he was not sure which way to proceed. If we went down the wrong way, we could end up a long way from the road. At that point, sharp cold needles of rain began to fall, making it still harder to see the way.

Taking Chandu's face in his hands, Dad looked deeply into our dog's eyes and said, "We're lost, Chandu. Find the car. Home, boy. Home."

Chandu looked into our faces. He sniffed the ground all around where we were standing. Then he raised his head and sniffed the late-afternoon scents.

"Go, Chan, take us home," Dad repeated.

Chandu wriggled under the fence as we climbed over. He moved ahead with Dad at his heels, Mom and me right behind, tightly holding hands. I was worried that we were lost, but I was more worried that Santa Claus might pass by our house if we were not safely home in bed that Christmas Eve!

How long it took us to stumble down that hillside and reach the road, I do not know. It felt like forever to me, a tired, frightened little girl. It was a slow trek following Chandu, because he stopped after every few steps to make certain we were with him. And just as we reached a small clearing between us and the fence bordering the road, Chandu's hackles rose, and he growled deeply.

Dad paused to look back, as twigs snapped and a noise that was a cross between a bellow and a snort came from the nearby thicket.

"Run!" Dad shouted. We heeded his word, sprinting to the fence and scrambling over in record time. Chandu halted, his fur bristling along his back, and barked fiercely at the beast trampling the underbrush. Safely in the roadway, we looked back to see the dim outline of a razorback hog at the brush line.

Chandu stood his ground until Dad called, "Come, Chandu!"

The dog glanced at us, now safely near the car. With a final volley of barks, he turned to obey, leaping easily over the fence. His tail wagging in a white-tipped blur, Chandu leaped up to lick our faces as we crowded around to hug and praise him.

The storm clouds moved on as swiftly as they had come, and the evening star appeared between them like a beacon. Dad squatted down beside the car to light his pipe, but not before I saw tears in his eyes as Chandu pressed against him momentarily. Chandu and I climbed into the backseat where, leaning our cold, damp bodies against each other, we were asleep almost before Dad turned on the car's ignition.

Dad and Mom often claimed that if they should get to the Pearly Gates and all the dogs and cats they had loved were not lined up to welcome them, they might not go in. If I should get there, and Chandu is not there to greet me, I, too, may just stand and wait for the dog that was my best pal and that saved us on that Christmas Eve so long ago.

## The Traditional Parade

by Linda Kaullen Perkins

The sparkle of the aluminum Christmas tree caught my eye before I crossed Ohio Street. Just yesterday, that same window of the J.C. Penney Store in Sedalia, Missouri, had an autumn display: two mannequins wearing plaid skirts, mohair sweaters, and penny loafers. Overnight, JoAnn, the talented window designer, had transformed the scene. The same two mannequins now wore high heels and silky blouses beneath wool suits. A Christmas tree, dotted with evenly spaced golden balls, towered over a stack of presents wrapped in red and gold foil with silver and crimson bows. I could imagine JoAnn whipping out the ribbon, looping it around her fingers a few times, and skillfully perfecting a huge bow. If only I could make bows like that.

"Mommy, look at that tree," a little girl shouted. She squeezed in front of me, pressing her nose to the window. "How does it do that?"

"Look over here." The woman said, her finger tapping the plate-glass window. "There's a color wheel turning. When the light shows through—see—it changes colors."

The little girl clapped her hands. She turned and looked at me, her blue eyes wide with wonder. "I like the green best."

I smiled. "I don't know which one I like best."

I glanced at my watch. *Better hurry, or I won't get clocked into work by 9:00 A.M.* A delicate snowflake drifted onto the sleeve of my cinnamon-colored suede jacket and stuck there like a miniature decoration. It was the first of many.

"Mommy, it's snowing," the little girl shrieked, spinning around and tipping her face heavenward.

Feathery snowflakes danced and swirled on the icy gusts of the north wind. My face tingled with a mixture of anticipation and chill. I smiled at the little girl's antics, then turned and wove through the crowd of people, making my way to the front door of the store.

Inside the recesses of the doorway, a crowd pressed together against the blast of winter. With shoulders hunched and collars pulled high, they waited for the store to open, puffing out conversations on frosty, white breaths.

"Excuse me," I said apologetically as I stepped in front of a lady wearing a black feathered hat. "I need to get to work."

I claimed a position in front of the door and glanced inside, spotting Jerry, the assistant manager, straightening ties by the door. We made eye contract. He nodded and then headed in my direction with a key. The latch clicked, and he shoved against the door.

"Good morning," he said to everyone within earshot. As soon as I slipped inside, he smiled at the crowd. "Won't be much longer, folks—only about eight more minutes."

"Quite a crowd today," I whispered as we moved past the racks of clothing and toward the middle of the store.

He stuffed the keys into his pocket and nodded. "I'm not surprised. The day of the Christmas parade is one of our best."

I hurried toward the shoe department and up the steps. Stopping on the balcony, I passed through the boys' department to enter the office and call, "Good morning, Ethel," before signing in.

I quickly got my cash drawer ready, then hurried past the racks of skirts and blouses, past the dressing rooms, and into the small room with the three-sided window. It had an excellent view of Third and Ohio streets. I looked up and down the streets and marveled at all the people who milled about, waiting for the parade to start.

"Morning, ladies," a voice boomed behind me.

*Was that my boss?*

I scurried out of the room to find Mr. Edwards, the manager, standing in the wide center aisle between the coats and dresses, with June, Thelma, and Betty gathered in front of him.

I eased in that direction, pretending to straighten merchandise along the way.

He looked at me, raised one eyebrow, and then continued with his speech. "Ladies, just want to remind you to be extra patient today," he said, his eyes darting from face to face. "And remember, the customer is always right."

I scrunched my toes inside my pointy shoes. Before the day was over, my feet would be hurting. Before I had a chance to lament the fact, footsteps pounded the staircase.

"Customers!" Mr. Edwards announced heartily, his face lighting up in a huge grin. Turning to us, he whispered, "May the Christmas Season of 1966 be a grand one!" As I recall, it was.

Though that particular Christmas parade marked the start of the holiday season some thirty-nine years ago, I remember it like it was just yesterday. Ohio and Main Street, adorned with huge, lighted candy canes, played center stage to area marching bands and beautiful floats. Retailers, with festive shop windows, anticipated crowds of excited shoppers filling their stores with smiling faces and open wallets. It was a glorious holiday. And though these days some things have changed, I take heart in the fact that some things haven't. Yes, it's true, nowadays Santa appears in September, and shoppers mostly pay for their purchases with plastic rather than cash, but the traditional Christmas parade still heralds the season. And no matter what else happens and how many things change, this particular gathering of people still has the ability to charm our community with the best holiday memories and dreams.

# A Charlie McCarthy Christmas

### by Renee Willa Hixson

I wanted a Charlie McCarthy doll with all my young heart. Each night, I dreamed of entertaining thousands of people with my ventriloquist talent. You could order them from the Sears & Roebuck Co. catalog for ten dollars. Unfortunately, my parents did not have that kind of money to spend on a present for me. There was barely twenty dollars for Christmas presents for all six of their children that year.

On the hour-long bus ride through the Ozark foothills to school each day, everyone talked about what they wanted for Christmas. The conversation was interrupted only when the bus stopped and children climbed out to run down paths and dirt roads toward their homes. Some houses were close to the road, and some were no more than small dwellings with tar-paper stapled to the outside.

Long bus rides to remote places where cash was scarce, if not nonexistent, gave each of us lots of time to think. There were no big houses. No fancy cars. The only beauty was in the gently rolling hills and the thick foliage that made the countryside famous. Still, we were not discouraged. No one really complained about being poor.

Our family didn't have a car and didn't go into town much, so we didn't do much window shopping. And like most of the kids in my school, we didn't even have a black-and-white television set. Most of our dreams were in our imaginations, which, as it turns out, was good for Mom and Grandma. I didn't know it at the time, but they were planning to make all our presents. Soft cotton dolls for my three sisters and me and wooden cars with thread-spool wheels for my two little brothers. Adequate presents for five uniformed little consumers like my siblings, perhaps, but not for me. While everybody else played in the woods after school, I studied my favorite page in my favorite book—the Sears & Roebuck Co. catalog. I only had eyes for the ventriloquist dolls. My heart's desire had black molded plastic hair and wore a black-and-white tuxedo.

Mom knew all about my obsession. She had lived through many previous career aspirations—a radio talk-show host, the first female fighter pilot. Now, I wanted to become a world-famous ventriloquist. It was my ticket to the mysterious land of television, which I had recently heard about. It was my ticket to a world away from the simple mountain life that seemed so small and drab to a young girl with a runaway imagination.

"You can't have everything that you want," said Mom. "At least not this year," she added quickly. "But don't give up your dream."

Crushed, I clutched the catalog to my chest and wandered around the cabin, bemoaning my fate. Unrequited dreams in a young child's mind can be so dramatic, but Mom was patient.

"Pray about it," she'd say as she gently stroked my blonde hair. "And then do something to keep your mind off of your disappointment—you never know what could happen."

*Never know?* Well, that's where my great imagination came to a screaming halt. We were poor. I thought that my dream was over.

As Christmas approached, school became very exciting. We sang Christmas songs at the beginning and end of each school day, pictures of Santa and his helpers plastered the classroom walls and lined the tiny school hall. One afternoon, three weeks before the holiday, the teacher made an announcement I will never forget.

"As you may be aware," she said, "the Ozark foothills are a poor area. Therefore, many families are unable to purchase Christmas presents for their children." The classroom filled with groans and disappointed sighs. She held up her hand for quiet and then smiled. "I am glad to announce that each student of this school will receive a voucher for $9! This voucher will be valid at any store in the town of Tahlequah. Merry Christmas!"

The room shook with cheers!

I sat at my desk, shivering with excitement. My dream was coming true! I could not wait to tell my mother. When the bus finally pulled up to our small dirt road, I flew out of the opened door and down the lane.

"Mom!" I yelled excitedly as I ran up the wooden stairs and into our little green cabin. "I'm gonna get my doll! I'm gonna be famous!"

Mom smiled wide and gave me a great big hug. "Everything works out," she said, uttering her favorite line. Still, I had to admit, she was right. Everything did work out. When we found out that no stores in Tahlequah sold ventriloquist dolls, Mom was not detoured. Instead, she took the last of the grocery money and ordered the doll from the catalogue. With my Christmas voucher, she bought toys for my preschool siblings.

I must confess that I did not become famous. I don't think I even achieved local celebrity status. The image of that smooth painted ventriloquist doll wearing a crisp black tuxedo has all but faded from my memory. But I still feel the magic. The wonder. The hope. And I will never forget the magical words of a mom, who lived in a small green cabin with six kids. She was right. Everything does work out.

On a Trade Wind

by Candy Killion

Old pirates who followed the currents to the island's rocky beaches were long gone, their bones mingled with natives who could not find rest below the sand, either, for the limestone was everywhere and unyielding. They called it Cayo Hueso then, "Bone Island." A rich Southerner mispronounced it, however, and it became Key West.

By December 1959, the islanders and visitors still assembled nightly at the water, not to sight the *Jolly Roger*, but to pause to watch the skies shimmer and melt into a color palette you could almost taste—smooth on the tongue like papaya. Holly-trimmed gingerbread frame-houses paled against the view from Mallory Square.

The Conch Train trolley, a year young and still fresh with paint, pulled up in time for the tanned young couple and their precocious daughter to watch the setting sun.

"Mommy! Look!" The child shrieked in delight. The child's mother stroked the little girl's hair, smiling.

"Pretty, huh?"

Vivid, sweeping pinks and oranges and purples reflected from the sky to the water, to the nodding child's clear hazel eyes.

"So, I am guessing this was a good idea, honey?" The man said as he sank to his knees on the sand, pretending to ask for forgiveness. His wife pushed him backward playfully.

"I hate to admit it, but you're right. But it doesn't exactly feel like Christmas," she said, then immediately clasped a hand over her mouth. As her husband brushed himself off, she whispered, "Little ears!"

Their daughter didn't miss a beat. "How will Santa know where I am? How will he bring my presents?" She asked just as the sun began its descent below the horizon, the happy colors fading away along with the child's Yuletide vacation hopes.

"Santa always finds a way, Sweet-pea. Always," her father said, taking her chubby hand in his. "In the meantime, it's time for ice cream."

Together they pressed up Duvall Street. Everywhere, men in Bermuda shorts, women in loose flowered dresses, and kids in shorts and sneakers laughed and looked in shop windows.

Scrunching her nose, the little girl tugged at her father's shorts. "Daddy?"

"Sweet-pea?"

"The Christmas music sounds—funny." Along the sidewalk, teenagers with bongo drums and guitars jammed to "Silent Night."

"Maybe not exactly funny, Sweet-pea. Different."

His wife chimed in. "You know the first 'Silent Night' was played on a guitar."

The child pondered that. "Okay. Like Elvis, right? But I still can't figure out how Santa is going to know."

Her father stopped laughing long enough to shoot his wife a discreet look of panic as he whisked them into the ice-cream parlor. A white-haired man, hefty and with a full snowy beard, leaning up against the bookshop storefront next door, reading a newspaper, heard the little girl mention her concerns about Santa Claus and approached.

He firmly shook the younger man's hand. "I couldn't help overhearing . . . if I may?"

When the father gave his permission, the older man looked down at the child.

"Young miss," he began, "I take it this is your first Christmas in Key West?" She nodded. "And you haven't heard about Santa and the pirates?"

"No," she said, her eyes round as marbles.

"Long ago—when pirates ruled the waters—people stood at the beach at sunset to see if any pirate ships were nearby. If not, they'd go to bed and sleep well that night."

"And if there were?" she asked.

"Then," he continued, "there would be a fight to keep the pirates away.

"One sunset, the people saw a pirate ship approaching. They were scared—and angry, too. It was Christmas Eve, certainly no time for pirates to be marauding around or spoiling things for the children."

He leaned closer and with a flourish continued his tale. "So they lit their lanterns and stayed at the dock, waiting for the pirates to come in, instead of waiting in pitch darkness. They sent the children to bed, and the fishermen and shopkeepers and the men who made fine cigars were there, people who used to live in places like England and Ireland and Cuba.

"For many of them, it was their children's first Christmas here. They wanted to make sure Santa could find them."

The little girl was mesmerized by the story. She could almost see the pirate ship in the distance and hoped it wouldn't show up this Christmas.

"The pirate ship came closer and closer, and still they kept their lanterns lit so Santa could find Key West."

"That was brave!" she offered.

"That it was—because the pirate ship could see them better, too."

Concern etched the child's face. "Then what happened?" She asked, almost afraid to hear the answer.

"Just as it seemed those pirates were going to anchor off the beach, the trade wind started blowin'—hard. And on it came the sound of sleigh bells, and almost out of nowhere came Santa. He landed his reindeer on deck, and they kicked, and they kicked, and they kicked some more, until every last pirate was in the water and swimming right back to where they came from!"

The child jumped up and clapped her hands in glee.

"And, Little Miss," he said with a smile, "Santa came to Key West that night, and he has come here every Christmas Eve since—on a trade wind. That's why all the street lanterns are lit up here, to make sure he remembers. And, that's also why you hear *Merry Christmas* and *Feliz Navidad* here, because the brave islanders who stood at the beach with their lanterns that night—well, that's how they all said Merry Christmas."

Back at the tiny guest house, Christmas Eve turned into Christmas morning, on a trade wind, just like the old man had said it would. There was a hula hoop, and a Betsy Wetsy, and even a copy of "The Purple People Eater." Everything the child had wanted.

Santa had found her.

Years later, the child, now grown, would sit in English class and view a snapshot of a beefy, white-haired writer who lived in Key West, a man who reminded her an awful lot of someone whom she had met in Key West many years before.

Christmas with Peppermint

by Candace Sams

*I*n 1968, my mother related a story to me that pertained to a simple yet very important Christmas tradition my grandfather had began way back in Palacios, Texas, in 1929. I have never forgotten her words.

During the Depression era, my grandfather and grandmother had twelve mouths to feed. When Christmas rolled around there wasn't much money for gifts, but there was one thing always present in the household. On Christmas Eve, after carols were sung around the tree, Grandpa brought out a huge candy cane. It was one of those arm-thick, red-and-white canes that you can still find in stores today, if you look hard enough.

Being a practical man, Grandpa would take an ordinary hammer and break apart the cane and hand everyone present a chunk of the candy. That was his Christmas gift to them.

Even to this day, my family doesn't celebrate Christmas without candy canes of some kind. My mom remembers times when fruit, nuts, and that peppermint were the only Christmas gifts that she and her siblings received. She remembers holding that chunk of peppermint in her hand more clearly than anything else that ever happened during the holidays. She remembers the smell of it, and how that scent brings back memories of a time when a man couldn't afford more for his kids than a broken piece of peppermint.

Mom has since received many nice gifts from my brothers and me. But she always remembers those holidays when she and her family had so little. She's taught me that some things are worth more than any costly gift from a fine store.

When I was a teenager, Grandpa still bought that big, foot-long candy cane, found his hammer, and whacked away at it so each of his grandchildren could have a piece. The significance was lost on me and my cousins. We used to laugh at him and make fun of what he was doing behind his back. None of us understood *doing without* because we were born in better times, and being handed a fistful of peppermint candy as a teenager wasn't our idea of a good gift. We've since learned otherwise.

Now, whatever store-bought gift my grandfather might have given me doesn't seem to matter so much as the warmth of that tradition.

I now celebrate Christmas each year with peppermint. I eat it on Christmas Eve in memory of my grandparents and of all my aunts and uncles who have since passed away. I eat it and think of times when others had less and I pretentiously thought I should have had more.

Today, my mother is all that is left of her once-large family. This Christmas, Mom will buy the foot-long peppermint stick the entire family will share. There won't be any laughter when the peppermint candy is passed around, though the teenagers in the bunch may snicker behind my mother's back. But some day, they, too, will have learned the importance of family ties and of remembering those who came before them. As we share this tradition with those coming after us, we can only hope the youngsters will remember the joy and deep satisfaction that our family discovered years ago in sharing a chunk of peppermint candy.

## What I Learned from a Child

by Joan Clayton

*I*n my first year of teaching, I commuted sixty-six miles a day to a wonderful little town called Texico, New Mexico. I didn't mind the drive because this little town's inhabitants made up the backbone of America. The parents bent over backward to help me, a budding teacher. Their family values and love of country made a permanent impression on me.

Growing up on farms made rosy cheeks and vigorous bodies. Plenty of cow's milk, cornbread and beans, home-canned fruits and vegetables, along with meat and eggs, built strong bones in my healthy third-grade students. Each day we went outside to play, regardless of the weather, and practically no one was absent the entire year.

My first lesson in America's heritage occurred when one student used the word *till* in his spelling sentence. "Put the money in the till." I had not the slightest hint of what that meant, but I soon learned he had used it correctly. Cash registers in those days were called "tills."

Looking back at my first year of teaching, I cherish the blessings that wonderful little community imparted to me. But, of all my memories from that wonderful little town, one stands out above all the others. It still brings tears and touches my heart. It was Christmas time—my third-graders couldn't wait until they could open their presents.

"Let's count to three," I said. Each of the children had brought in a gift either for a boy or for a girl, and I had already done a silent head count to be sure there was a gift for each of the children.

"ONE, TWO, THREE!" I shouted. The oohs and ahhs heard from children opening gifts plus the exuberance and excitement warmed my heart.

"Look what I got!" said one.

"Wow, this is just what I wanted!" said another.

I became a child again as I walked around my classroom joining in the enthusiasm so contagious in children. I waited until everyone had seen all the presents, giving them time to enjoy each one.

"Now, it's my turn," I said. "Everyone close your eyes while I pass out your gifts from me." Quietness settled over the room as twenty-five little cherubs put their heads down.

"Don't peek," I added as I placed a carefully wrapped package in front of each child. I saw peeking eyes all over the place. Some looked between their arms, while others pretended with half-shut eyes.

When I had handed out the last gift, I stepped back. "I'm ready. Open your eyes!" Shouts of joy echoed over the room. They tore away the paper in seconds and emptied the contents from the decorated packages. Who would have thought that a new tablet, a box of crayons, new pencils, a book, some candy canes, and a simple toy could have given so much pleasure?

Immediately, the little angels swept toward me with hugs and thank-yous.

Later that day, as I dismissed the children for the Christmas vacation, I noticed Timmie working diligently on something with his new crayons. I reminded him not to miss the bus.

"I'm almost finished," he said with a twinkle in his eye. After a few more marks with his crayon, Timmie handed me a sheet of paper from his new tablet. "Here, Teacher, this is for you. We didn't have the money to buy a present for you so I made something. I hope you like it."

Timmie had spent the last part of his party time working on this special gift. Tears filled my eyes as I saw what he had drawn. It was a picture of the two of us, holding hands. On the paper, he'd written: "Mrs. Clayton and Timmie." Little red hearts filled the empty spaces. The bottom of his paper contained these words in bold letters: "I Give You Me!"

What better gift could I ever receive from an adoring child? He had given me a gift filled with unconditional love from him to me. I saw Jesus in that lovable little person, and I understood one more time the whole reason for Christmas. That memory reminds me that there is more to the holiday than meets the eye.

*What can I give to the Christ Child? What can I give to the one who came to earth to save me from eternal destruction?* I have nothing that is worthy of the King of Kings. I cannot work, give, or even earn such a precious gift. In the light of the great sacrifice, his death on the cross . . . there is only one thing I can do.

Like my student, I want to draw a picture of me holding hands with God. On it I would write: "I Give You Me!"

# The Best Christmas Ever

by Marcia Rudoff

We didn't celebrate Christmas—not really. My sister and brothers and I, during the Santa Claus–believing years, would hang our stockings from the fireplace mantel and find them filled with candies and nuts, an orange in each toe for filler. There was no tinsel-laden tree sheltering brightly wrapped gifts, no new toys, no wreath on the door. We were Jewish, after all.

This was the 1930s, long before Chanukah was discovered by Hallmark and Hasbro and elevated to equal commercial holiday status. The Chanukah of my childhood was a minor Jewish holiday, commemorated by the lighting of skinny little orange candles over an eight-day period, eating potato pancakes, and playing a special game with a four-sided top, called a dreidel, that had a different Hebrew letter on each of its four sides. Depending on which side the top landed on, you got to put or take pennies or candies into or out of the "pot." Gifts, one each night, given out after the lighting of the candles, could range from real money, like a shiny dime, or chocolate candy coins wrapped in gold paper. That was it.

Sing all the songs you want about lighting candles and making dreidels out of clay, it still wasn't Christmas. While the neighborhood kids sported their new bikes, sleds, or winter finery, I could only sigh within over my peculiar faith that excluded me from Christmas.

The letters on the Chanukah dreidel stand for "A great miracle happened there." One year, when I was about four, a miracle really did happen in our house: We had Christmas! Not a sensible new winter coat, pajamas, and socks Christmas, but toys, toys, and more toys Christmas.

It was night, almost bedtime, but my father wasn't home yet. He seemed to be working extra late. Then we heard voices on the porch. The door opened and there he was, rolling a light gray doll carriage, just my size, into the room. Behind him was a man I'd never seen before, carrying a large stuffed elephant, big enough for my baby brother to sit on. He put it down beside the carriage and went out again with my father, only to return with still more surprises, a dizzying progression of dolls and trucks and stuffed animals that my older sister and brother were eagerly pouncing on.

I took possession of the carriage, wheeling it around the room and placing one of the smaller dolls my sister hadn't claimed yet inside. I climbed back onto the couch beside my mother, my treasure parked in front of me. I watched my father and the stranger, too tall and thin and young to be Santa Claus but acting like he was, going in and out of our house, returning each time with more toys. The living room was filling up, my sister and brothers were playing with everything, laughing, excited, and I sat stunned, trying to take it all in, to believe it was happening.

Then the stranger was in front of me, kneeling down, handing me a stuffed toy, a white doggy with a rubber tube in his mouth. Attached to the tube was a small baby bottle filled with water. As I cradled the toy dog, the man pinched its tail and the water drained out of the bottle into the animal. It was drinking! I smiled up at the man, and he smiled back. He took my hand and showed me how to squeeze the water back into the bottle. I sat happily making my doggy drink and regurgitate. It was magic, like this whole night.

I felt my mother get up from the couch. She was at the door now with my father and the nice man. I remember his face. I didn't know anyone could look that sad and happy at the same time. He was watching us, lost in play, while talking quietly at the door with my parents. He shook hands with my father and nodded as my mother gave him a goodbye hug. His face, over her shoulder, seemed to be fighting back tears. Then he was gone, and as my parents turned from the door, I could see my mother was crying too. My father was shaking his head from side to side with his lips pressed tightly together, the way he did when something bad happened. I couldn't understand it. Here we were, the most wonderful, amazing night of our lives and my parents are acting like someone had died. How could they be sad with all this happiness?

Years later, of course, I understood. When the Great Depression took its toll on other clients of my father's and their businesses too failed, we acquired porch furniture that had once graced the verandah of a local resort, a pinball machine from a boardwalk arcade, other odd items from a variety of shops. There was no money. We were living on the barter system. My father did the dentist's books and tax returns; he cared for our teeth. My father did the doctor's books and tax returns; he treated our measles and chicken pox. We shopped for clothes and shoes only at clients' stores. The town survived. When businesses went under, they liquidated inventory their way, to settle as best they could with those they owed, before the banks and auctioneers moved in.

And that is why the toy store proprietor, his own Christmas dreams collapsing along with his business, urged his equally struggling accountant to accept as payment all the toys he would have liked to give his children, if only he had the money.

I don't know what became of the toy-store owner. I don't even know if that night was actually Christmas Eve, but to my child's mind, what other night could it possibly be? This "Santa" didn't hold his belly and say "Ho, ho, ho," but from our frenzied joy, he did find within him a smile, probably the last he would have for many bad days ahead.

Perhaps we gave him a Christmas present too.

Secondhand Happiness

by Esther M. Bailey

In 1940 my family moved from the farm to Fredericktown, Ohio. That was quite a change for an eleven-year-old. To me, a town with a population of 2,000 people was big-city living. I could walk to school instead of waiting for a bus to pick me up. Any time my mother was fresh out of eggs or milk, I could run to the store for her. As an only child, I also enjoyed getting together with friends after school. Both of my parents worked so the town offered a variety of things to do. No longer did I have to entertain myself with a book.

Then came Christmas. For the first time I missed the farm, where my dad and I trekked to the woods to cut down a Christmas tree. "Don't worry," my dad said. "I'll buy you a Christmas tree." His assurance satisfied me for the moment because Dad had never let me down. From the first of December, I started looking for the Christmas tree to arrive. This year I would be able to help with the decorating more than in years past. What fun it would be to string popcorn, hang the strips of aluminum foil representing icicles, and place the prettiest ornaments where they would show best. I often rehearsed the big event in my mind.

A week or two later I asked my dad, "When will we get a Christmas tree?"

"I'm not sure but we'll get one."

Night after night I watched for my father's homecoming— each time without a Christmas tree.

Finally, it was Christmas Eve. It's now or never, I thought. Pressing my nose against the window, I wanted to get the first glimpse of Dad carrying a Christmas tree. Finally, he came into sight with his head bowed and empty arms. My father avoided me with his eyes as he entered the house. I went to my room to nurse my hurt. At the time, I did not understand that Christmas meant more than decorations and presents.

While trapped in my misery, I overheard my parents talking in low voices. I strained to listen. "But I promised Esther a Christmas tree," Dad said.

The pain in my father's voice touched my heart, and I immediately transferred my pain to concern for my Dad. Without trying to find out the reason for the missing tree, a plan formed in my mind.

A few moments later, I left my room with a smile on my face. Approaching my parents, I said, "Dad, could we get down those two little artificial Christmas trees?" I remembered seeing them among the decorations the year before.

The action required to comply with my request seemed to soften the lines of stress on my father's face. With feigned enthusiasm, I began the decorating process. Two pine trees about twelve inches tall didn't offer many artistic options, but I made quite a display of draping tinsel around the tiny branches. Even the smallest ornaments dwarfed the trees, but I acted as though I had created a masterpiece.

If my father knew I was pretending, he never let on. Soon his spirits lifted, and our family began to enjoy a memorable Christmas Eve. Although I did not experience a dramatic moment when joy overwhelmed me, at some point I realized that I no longer needed to put on an act. In trying to cheer up my dad, I had captured happiness for myself.

Santa's Reluctant Helper

by Linda Rondeau

Wiping the sleep from my eyes, I saw my little girl squatting and looking eye to eye at the packaged item standing under the Christmas tree. It was four in the morning, and I had no idea how long she had been there.

We had joined my parents for a country Christmas at their home in Burke where my father and mother had moved only a few years before, shaking off the dust of the city and returning to the roots of their childhood. I was grateful for the toys and clothes Mother had bought the children. She had set a few unwrapped items under the tree before retiring to bed, doing her bit to keep the fantasy of Santa alive for another year—a magnanimous gesture for one who so despised the myth.

If it had not been for her, my children would have wondered if Santa cared about them. Divorced, unemployed, and with a scant amount of support money, what little allowance I received from the government barely paid for rent and food.

Outside of crayons and coloring books, Christmas, as I hoped it would be, was out of the question.

Mother understood my heartache. A child of the Depression, she herself had known many disappointing Christmases and hoped to provide better for her own children; but, it was not until Christmas 1948 that she first began to actually despise Santa. "Santa Claus is a cruel hoax for poor children," she'd said time and time again.

The years following World War II were difficult for returning vets. Jobs were scare and finding shelter for their families a daunting task. The only housing my parents could afford was in the south side of the city. They rented a cold-water flat, the euphemism given to apartments with no hot running water. Rodents of all kinds found their way into the cleanest of these dwellings. They would eat anything, even gnawing their way through aluminum garbage cans. Fearful that the rats would bite her children, Mother spent many sleepless nights vigilantly listening for any sounds that might indicate danger. She longed for the day when the countryside would take her back to a place where she no longer knew the fear generated by four-legged city dwellers.

A child of the Depression and a wife of a returning soldier, Mother was grateful for her surroundings, grateful that her family was all together under one roof even if money was scarce. My father's factory paycheck paid the rent and bought food—leaving little for luxuries of any kind, especially events like Christmas. I was still a baby, unaware that there was a special day to be excited about. My brother, on the other hand, had been looking forward to Christmas and to Santa's showering of presents for all good boys and girls.

At first, my brother was thrilled when he opened the holster gun set and cowboy hat under the tree. "Oh, boy! I'm a real cowboy, now!" He flitted about the house shooting bad men who lurked behind the couch and chair. Then he took his treasure outside. It was not long before he rushed back into the house, his countenance forever changed. "Have I been good, Mom?" my brother asked.

"Of course, you have," Mother reassured him.

"Then why did Santa Claus only bring me two presents? Santa brought Danny ten presents and a new bike?"

My mother didn't know how to answer his child spirit. How could she explain poverty to a four-year-old, an innocent who didn't know he was poor? Mother took the fall for Santa.

"Well, honey," she ventured to explain. "Moms and dads have to pay Santa for the presents. We didn't have very much money to give him." She watched helplessly as her child faced the brutal realities of social inequities for the first time in his life, knowing the experience would be repeated many times over.

As I watched, the snow fall gently on the blue spruce, far away from the squalor of city life, I knew Mother understood the heartache I felt that Christmas. My three-year-old turned to look at me, eyes filled with tears. "For me?" she asked, not quite believing it might be true.

"Yes, honey. Santa brought it for you."

I helped her remove the cellophane wrapping. She hugged the treasured gift so tightly, her little fingers turned white.

"It's just what I wanted! He remembered!"

"Yes, he remembered."

In my heart, I was grateful to a mother whose memory reached from her pain and gave comfort.

Daddy's Christmas Dinner

by Betty Koffman

Growing up in the 1950s, I was aware that my mother was always busy, working at home, or contributing to family income by clerking in a ladies' clothing shop, but always making our house a warm place to be, especially during the holidays from Thanksgiving to Christmas.

Our family enjoyed holiday meals gathered around the dining table, rehashing old stories and catching up on news of different relatives. Grandma and Grandpa and Uncle Pat, who was unmarried, came from Virginia, and sometimes Uncle Claude and his wife would come from Kentucky.

My mother was there, an apron tied around her waist, putting the turkey stuffed with cornbread dressing in to roast early in the morning, later preparing the vegetables, bowls of mashed potatoes, green beans, slaw, corn, sweet potato casserole, along with gravy and cranberry sauce, and pans of hot rolls. Pumpkin and pecan pies had been made the day before. I helped set the table and fill the water glasses.

The Christmas I was twelve was different. I knew something was wrong when I came home from my friend Linda's house one day, and found Daddy and Bill pawing through the box of Christmas ornaments, faces downcast. They were quiet, and Mother was lying down. I sniffed the fragrant cedar tree. "What's the matter?"

Bill spoke first. "Mother has to have surgery. She won't be home for Christmas." He hung a silver ball on the tree.

I stared at him. Was this a joke? A trick? Mother had to be there for Christmas.

"You're kidding, aren't you? Besides, who would cook dinner?"

Daddy said, "It's no joke, honey."

I sat beside him on the sofa, and he hugged me close. "Your mother has to have her gall bladder removed, and we'll all have to help."

"She'll be all right, won't she? She's not going to die?"

Daddy kissed me on the cheek. "She'll be fine, but she won't be home for Christmas." He plucked some ornaments from the box and stood up.

"But, Daddy, what about the turkey?" Bill said.

Daddy grinned for the first time. "I guess I'll have to do it."

I said, "You don't ever cook anything."

Daddy hung a toy clown on the tree. "Well, how hard can it be to roast a turkey?"

Bill and I looked at each other and rolled our eyes.

On Christmas Eve, we went to see Mother in the hospital and took her a poinsettia in a pot with red foil around it. She was pale and weak, but she looked pretty in her pink bed jacket. Her reddish-blonde hair was brushed. She hugged us kids and winked at Daddy when we told her he was going to cook Christmas dinner.

"Save me some turkey and dressing," she said sleepily, closing her eyes.

Bill smothered a giggle. We'd already decided that we'd probably have hamburgers for dinner. That was the only thing Daddy ever made besides homemade ice cream.

We were up early Christmas morning to open presents. It was cold and gray, but the snow we wished for hadn't fallen. Daddy sat in the kitchen reading the paper and drinking coffee. After we finished tearing into the packages, I noticed the oven was warm and asked Daddy what was cooking.

"Guess somebody put a turkey into roast." He ducked behind the newspaper, but not before I saw him grin.

Bill whispered, "Maybe we can eat at Kelly and Pete's house." Kelly was a friend of our mother and a great cook.

"We can't hurt Daddy's feelings. Besides, Grandma and Grandpa will be here."

Bill sighed. "Let's play Monopoly until dinner's ready."

After a while, Daddy came in dressed in his brown suit. "Time to set the table and get cleaned up. Grandma and Grandpa and Uncle Pat will be here soon, and dinner's almost ready."

Daddy hung his jacket on a chair and went off to the kitchen. Pots and pans clanked. Bill snickered, "I can't wait to see this."

After we set the table, I put on my new plaid skirt and sweater and brushed my dark hair. Bill wore new jeans and a pullover. Grandma and Grandpa and Uncle Pat pulled up in their old Ford. Daddy held the door open for them.

In a little while, Daddy hollered, "Time to eat!"

The grownups went first. Suddenly Bill burst out, "Wow!"

I pushed him aside. "What is it?"

A poinsettia and red candles sat in the center of the white tablecloth. In front of Daddy's chair was a huge golden brown turkey with cornbread stuffing spilling out on the platter. My mouth flew open.

Daddy's green eyes sparkled; then Grandpa said the blessing. We prayed for Momma to get well fast. Daddy sliced the turkey, spooned on dressing, and passed plates around. Bowls of vegetables and warm rolls circled the table, and knives and forks clinked. Tender white meat melted in my mouth.

Nobody talked for a while. Then Bill leaned back moaning, "That was pretty good. I never thought . . . "

I kicked him under the table, and he finished, ". . . I didn't know you could cook."

Everybody laughed, and Daddy said, "There are a lot of things you don't know."

I said, "I really miss Momma, but this is just about the best Christmas dinner we've ever had." I clapped a hand over my mouth. "Oh, don't tell her I said that."

We all laughed again, and when Daddy brought out pie with real whipped cream, I thought my stomach would burst.

Daddy never let us forget that we had doubted him and always teased Momma that his turkey was better than hers. She let him believe it.

Silver-Dollar Christmas

by Marian Webster

𝓘 wasn't born there, but if someone asks me the name of my hometown, without hesitation I reply Kingman, Arizona. Kingman has changed drastically with the passage of the years, but to those of us who grew up there in the 1940s, there is no place like home. We roamed freely and without fear from one end of town to the other, walking everywhere without complaint. Social status and home addresses were no barriers to friendships from the south side beyond the railroad tracks to the north side on the hills behind the courthouse, from the east side where Route 66 wound upward to Hilltop, to the west side where the high school and swimming pool were. Just like the song says, "Get your kicks on Route 66 Flagstaff, Arizona, and don't forget Winona, Kingman, Barstow, San Bernardino." And that's where Dad's small service station and garage was, right on old Route 66 in Kingman, Arizona.

Life hadn't been easy for Mom and Dad. Dad had been plagued all his adult life by chronic eye problems. Suddenly, without warning, in late 1949 a ruptured blood vessel left him with only poor vision in one eye. He was forced to sell the auto salvage business he had owned for many years and the home he had built for his family at the junction where the railroad tracks separated to continue their way eastward and southward. Life changed drastically for us after that. Childhood was over, and my brothers and I went our separate ways into adulthood. Now, when I return to Kingman, I drive by the old home site, where nothing remains but the crumbling cement foundation of our house, almost hidden by the overgrown weeds. Memories of growing up there still seem to emanate from the ruins.

Dad worked at whatever he could find to do, and Mom went to work as a telephone operator. Then Mom was diagnosed with breast cancer, resulting in a total mastectomy, and later Dad developed the heart trouble that plagued him for the rest of his life. With no medical insurance, keeping their heads above water financially was a constant struggle. But in spite of his ill health, Dad managed to get that small service station and garage on Route 66. And no matter how difficult life was, they saved for a rainy day. And that's where the story of the silver dollars begins.

Travelers who had hit it lucky in Las Vegas would stop at Dad's service station to fill up their gas tanks, and sometimes they paid their bill with their silver-dollar winnings. The silver dollars went to Mom, and quietly she hoarded them away, saving them for something special. And that Christmas of forty-five years ago was something very special. Their children were coming home, bringing their families with them. For the first time, the whole family would be together for Christmas.

Christmas Eve meant that Mom had her usual pot of chili simmering on the stove, ready for anyone who might happen to drop in or for any of her family who made it home for Christmas. Her system of cooking the Christmas turkey was simple: she put it into a slow-cooking oven just before she went to bed on Christmas Eve, and then she prayed, asking God to wake her up when the turkey was done. Her system never failed, even the time that she woke up much earlier than expected and lay there arguing with God, convinced that the turkey couldn't be done yet. But unable to return to sleep, she got up and checked the turkey. It was, as always, cooked to perfection. That was one thing about Mom—she and God were in a one-on-one personal relationship no matter how difficult life became.

Mom spent her cache of silver dollars that Christmas. She and Dad paid for presents for all her children and grandchildren and for a Christmas dinner unequaled in perfection. A family photo shows a happy bunch. The little boy cousins had been transformed into little cowboys, complete with the pistol and holster sets their Granny had bought them. Cousins met cousins for the first time and, in some cases, for the only time.

That Christmas with Mom and Dad in our hometown became even more special with the passage of years. It turned out to be the only time we were all together as a family. It was, in every way, truly a silver-dollar Christmas.

# Contributors

**Georgia Aker** ("Searching for the Holiday") is Texas born, but she has spent most of her nearly ninety years in New Mexico, the last thirty as a rancher's wife. In 1998, shortly after Georgia was widowed the second time, she moved to Fresno, California, where she currently lives with her daughter and husband. In addition to doing most of the cooking, she has mentored several students in English as a second language, is active in her church, is a freelance writer, and travels as often as possible.

**Barbara Anton** ("The Gift of a Brother") has received more than 200 writing awards. She has had two books published: *Terse Verse* and *Savories*, a collection of short stories, as well as many articles. Barbara teaches writing at the University of South Florida, Senior Division, and has written columns for newspapers and writer's magazines.

**Trish Ayers** ("The Christmas Angel") has been a resident of Berea, Kentucky, for twenty-one years. She discovered her life's purpose of writing while learning to live with a chronic illness. Recently, her work has been published in *Poetry as Prayer*, *Appalachian Women Speak*, and *The Rocking Chair Reader: Memories from the Attic*. Her play, *LUMPs*, is part of the first Kentucky Women's Playwright Festival. Many of her plays have been produced domestically and internationally, including plays specifically written for Mountain Spirit Puppets.

**Esther M. Bailey** ("Secondhand Happiness") moved to Detroit in 1955, where she met and married her husband, Ray. In 1972, the Baileys sold their tool business and moved to Phoenix, Arizona, where they now reside.

**Nancy Baker** ("Christmas Warmth") resides in College Station, Texas, with her husband of forty-six years. After retiring from Texas A&M University, Nancy pursued her lifelong love of writing and has been published in national magazines and various anthologies. She directs the ministry to the sick program at her church and is a hospice volunteer.

**Barbara Brady** ("Making the Magic Last"), a retired registered nurse, lives in Topeka, Kansas, with her husband of almost fifty years. She enjoys church, sunflowers, books, volunteer activities, and—most of all—her family and friends. Barbara is the author of *A Variety of Gifts*, *Smiling at the Future*, and *Seasoned with Salt*. Her work has been published in various markets.

**Sylvia Bright-Green** ("A Truly Memorable Christmas") has been writing for twenty-six years and has published more than 560 articles, columns, and short stories in local and national publications. She has been published in two Adams Media books series, A *Cup of Comfort* and *The Rocking Chair Reader*, as well as in the *Famous Wisconsin Mystics* book, and a state historical book. She also hosted a talk show and teaches at conferences and colleges in her home state of Wisconsin.

**Marcia E. Brown** ("The Dog Saved the Day"), freelance writer in Austin, Texas, is pleased to preserve family stories, especially for her grandson. Since 1993, her work has appeared regularly in magazines, newspapers, and anthologies, including the *Cup of Comfort* and *Rocking Chair Reader* series. Several of her stories have won awards. She is currently seeking agent representation for her humorous memoir, *Mamas Don't Grow on Trees*.

**Dorothy L. Bussemer** ("No Room for You, Either") is an eighty-three-year-old senior citizen, now retired from the federal government, Department of Defense. She has a college degree in social science and a minor in economics. Dorothy has been writing since 1996, and she has had more than 350 stories and poems published.

**Lesa Cameron** ("Do You See What I See?") is a former library director turned freelance writer whose work has appeared in such periodicals as *Nebraskaland, American*

*Libraries, the Boy Scout Leader Magazine,* and *Holt International Families.* A winner in the 2005 Bess Streeter Aldrich Short Story Contest, Lesa resides in the Village of Greenwood, Nebraska, with her husband and two children.

**Kathe Campbell** ("Christmas Blues") and her husband, Ken, live on a 7,000-foot mountain near Butte, Montana, where they have raised national champion spotted asses. They have three grown children and eleven grandchildren. Kathe has contributed to newspapers and national magazines on Alzheimer's disease, and she has had her work published in various anthologies.

**Guy Carrozzo** ("Thank You, Miss Farley") was born in McKeesport, Pennsylvania, in 1932. His family moved to Hawthorne, California, in 1946. He served four years in the U.S. Air Force, and thirty years in education: five years as a teacher and twenty-five years as a principal. Guy has two adult children and four grandchildren. He has been married for fifty years.

**J. Hogan Clark** ("Sam"), a former employee of the Office of Naval Intelligence, is active in community affairs in Sedalia, Missouri, where he currently lives. In addition, Jack is a freelance writer and songwriter and enjoys spending his free moments on the front porch strumming on an acoustic guitar.

**Nan B. Clark** ("A Treasure Unspent") was born and raised in New Hampshire, and although she now lives in Beverly, Massachusetts, on Boston's North Shore, she still laments the loss of the Old Man of the Mountain, whose granite face crumbled into dust after fascinating artists and writers, including her soul mate Nathaniel Hawthorne, for centuries.

**Joan Clayton** ("What I Learned from a Child") is a retired educator of thirty-one years. She and her husband reside in Portales, New Mexico. Joan's passion is writing and her husband's is ranching. They have three sons and six grandchildren. Joan is presently working on her latest book. Visit her Web site at *www.joanclayton.com.*

**Jeanne Converse** ("A Small Town Christmas Story") is a freelance writer. Her book, *How to Organize Your Household in One Hour per Day*, was published in 2002. She also has written various articles and short stories for magazines, newspapers, and print anthologies.

**Nancy Jo Eckerson** ("Three Giant Wise Men") is a freelance writer located in western New York. She is also the assistant to the town historian, John Eckerson. Nancy is a devoted fan of romance and reminiscence, and to this day, remains an adoring fan of her dad.

**Norma Favor** ("Handfuls of Pennies") lives in the mountains of Idaho. She loves to write about her ancestors. Twenty-two grandchildren fill the rest of her spare time.

**John R. Gugel** ("The Giving Season") is a freelance author and minister on disability leave. His most recent book is titled *Cries of Faith, Songs of Hope: Prayers for the Times of Our Life*. He and his wife, Linda, have three grown children: Jeremy, Jessica, and Nathan.

**Shirley P. Gumert** ("The Gift of a Smile") is a freelance writer who lives in West Kerr County, Texas. She has written articles and columns for the *Santa Fe* (New Mexico) *Reporter*, several other New Mexico newspapers, the *Houston Chronicle's Texas Magazine*, and *The Rocking Chair Reader: Coming Home*.

**Lynn R. Hartz** ("The Costume") lives in Charleston, West Virginia. Her stories have appeared in *A Cup of Comfort for Christmas* and *Small Miracles for Families*. She has authored three books: *And Time Stood Still*, the story of the midwife who delivered the Christ Child; *Club Fed: Living in a Women's Prison*; and *Praise Him in Prison*.

**Julie Bonn Heath** ("The Giving Year") is the compiler of *Then Along Came an Angel: Messengers of Deliverance*. Julie teaches writing/marketing classes online and at writer's conferences nationwide and owns a marketing company, *www.astepaheadmarketing.com*.

**M. DeLoris Henscheid** ("I Married Santa Claus"), the sixth of eight consecutive generations of women in her family who have lived in Blackfoot, Idaho, is the mother of nine grown children. DeLoris received her B.A. in early childhood education from Idaho State University, taught kindergarten for eight years, and since retirement, has been active in the Idaho Writer's League, concentrating on stories of the women in her family.

**Debbie Hill** ("Miracle on Rolling Acres Drive") has four grown children and nine grandchildren. Debbie loves family, arts and crafts, and her newest passion: writing. She is operations manager for an industrial supply and steel company and has always lived in South Texas where the weather is hot and humid—most of the time.

**Charlotte A. Hilliard** ("The Christmases of My Youth") has been published in *Reminisce Magazine, The East Texas Peddler, The Newton News*, and *The Kirbyville Banner*. To fulfill her wish to tell the stories of the people who lived in the community she grew up in, Charlotte started writing three years ago and is thoroughly enjoying it.

**Renee Willa Hixson** ("A Charlie McCarthy Christmas" and "The Sainted Arm of the Holiday Season") moved frequently as a young girl, and saw a great deal of small-town America. Now she is the mother of four children and a freelance writer. She has published a series of stories for an early-childhood education curriculum and has taught high school English.

**Joyce McDonald Hoskins** ("The Half-Priced Puppy") is a long time resident of Stuart, Florida, and is a full-time freelance writer. When not writing Joyce works in her garden and spends time with her pets, a small dog and a huge cat.

**Janet M. Hounsell** ("My Father") is a retired full-time newspaper photo/journalist and the author of a town history. She now keeps busy freelancing and providing four area newspapers with regular columns. Janet's book, *The Geezer Book of Tips and Nostalgia,* is soon to be published.

**Janet Anderson Hurren** ("Hard Times") taught International Baccalaureate World Literature, among other things, at Bonn American High School in Germany, before moving to Virginia. After her husband retired from the CIA, they moved to Brigham City, Utah, where they remain. In addition to working as a teacher, Janet has been a banker and a litigation specialist.

**Joan Rawlins Biggar Husby** ("Christmas Card from My Sister") grew up in the logging community of Robe, Washington. She taught school, raised two children, and now writes articles, poetry, and books. Presently, she is writing family history essays.

**Marilyn Jaskulke** ("Poke-and-Plum Town") is a published writer, her work appearing in several inspirational anthologies and other Christian publications. Originally from Minnesota, she resides with her husband in Mission Viejo, California. She is a mother of four sons, grandmother to eleven, and great-grandmother of two. She spends long hours sewing quilts for her family and for the mission field, as a member of Grace and Peace Quilts.

**Jewell Johnson** ("Christmas Caroling") lives in Arizona with her husband, LeRoy. They have six grown children and eight grandchildren. Besides writing, Jewell spends her time walking, reading, and quilting.

**Judith Bader Jones** ("Christmas Sequins") is a poet, short fiction writer, and photographer. Her works have appeared in literary and commercial publications including *The Kansas City Star, The Same, Buffalo Spree*, and many others. She is a poetry editor for *Kansas City Voices.*

**Candy Killion** ("On a Trade Wind") is a freelance writer who has appeared in *The Rocking Chair Reader* series, is a chapter contributor to Atriad Press' *Haunted Encounters* anthology series, and *Chicken Soup for the Healthy Living Soul: Menopause*. She lives in southeast Florida, within easy reach of Key West's trade winds.

**Mimi Greenwood Knight** ("The Box") is a freelance writer. Her essays and articles have appeared in *Parents Magazine*, *Working Mother, American Baby, Christian Parenting Today, Campus Life, Sesame Street Parents, Bottom Line Personal, At-Home Mother,* and *Mothers at Home,* as well as in several anthologies. More about Mimi at: *www.writergazette.com.*

**Betty Koffman** ("Daddy's Christmas Dinner") a native of Kentucky, grew up in eastern Tennessee in the foothills of the Smoky Mountains. Betty, who has a degree in English from East Tennessee State University, lives and writes in Kingsport.

**Catherine Lanser** ("The Great Walnut Caper") lives in Madison, Wisconsin. She grew up in Port Washington, Wisconsin, the youngest in a family of nine children, and she enjoys writing about that time in her life.

**Patti Mattison Livingston** ("Before Portland") was born in Medford, Oregon, but her childhood unfolded across the states of Oregon, Arizona, and California—wherever her father's job took them. In 1944, she married Clarence Livingston, her high school sweetheart, who was a pilot in the Marine Corps. After World War II, they moved to Claremont, California, to raise lemons, and rear four children—all in one place—before moving to Egypt for seven years, prior to Clarence's retirement. Now widowed, Patti spends her days writing and remembering.

**Helen Luecke** ("One Bright Night") lives in Amarillo, Texas, with her husband, Richard. She is cofounder of the Amarillo Chapter of Inspirational Writers Alive! She writes short stories, articles, and devotionals.

**Michelle Mach** ("Grandma's Gift") lives in Fort Collins, Colorado. Her work has appeared in *Simple Pleasures of Friendship, KnitLit 3*, and *ByLine Magazine.*

**Dianne Neal Matthews** ("The Perfect Gift") writes articles, devotionals, poetry, and newspaper articles. In addition, she has completed a one-year devotional book entitled *On This Day,* which was released in fall 2005.

**Sandra McGarrity** ("Scarves and Popcorn") has been published in several anthologies including but not limited to the *God Allows U-Turns* series and *House Blessings*. She has also written for such magazines as *Virtue, Personal Journaling, Learning Through History*, and others. Sandra resides in Chesapeake, Virginia, and is the author of two novels.

**Terri Meehan** ("A Christmas to Cherish" and "Shared Memories") was born and raised in Ohio. Currently, she resides in London, England, with her British husband, John. Terri currently works for legal publishers in London. In her spare time, she writes articles for various Christian books and Web sites.

**Joyce Anne Munn** ("From the Heart") taught elementary school for thirty-nine years and loved every minute of it. Currently, Joyce volunteers for several community activities and also serves on the national board of Christian Educators Association International, an organization for public school teachers.

**Lee Ann Sontheimer Murphy** ("Home for the Holidays") is a freelance writer and a native of St. Joseph, Missouri. Currently, she lives and writes on a rocky ridge in the Ozarks with her husband, three children, and assorted pets. She is a member of the Missouri Writers Guild, and she was the recipient for the 2005 Editor's Pen Award from the literary journal *Scrivener's Pen*.

**Phyllis Nagle** ("The Best Party Ever"), active alumnus of the University of California, Berkeley, and long-time resident of the San Francisco Bay Area, resides with her husband in Alamo. Her greatest pleasure is time spent with their five young grandchildren. She is a member of Wednesday Writers Group in Oakland, California, which raised funds for breast cancer research with their book of essays. Phyllis, a member of the California Writers Club, has contributed to the local Knight Ridder publication.

**Mary Jane Nordgren** ("Make-Believe World") retired from teaching to make her way through medical school with her three small children. After retiring from family practice in Forest Grove, Oregon, she and her logger husband built a home on a hill overlooking the Cascade Range to write and to gather the children and grandchildren for love and laughter.

**Joseph Pantatello** ("On a Wish and a Sled") is retired and has been writing for several years. His stories have appeared in the small press, anthologies, and have won awards in major contests. Joseph likes to write fantasy and mystery, and a little romance to please his wife, Caroline.

**Linda Kaullen Perkins** ("The Traditional Parade"), free-lance writer and novelist, has had articles published in several local newspapers. Currently, she contributes a monthly selection of short stories to *Party Line,* a local magazine. After retiring in 2001 after thirty-one years as an elementary school teacher, Linda completed a 70,000-word historical manuscript. She is a member of Romance Writers of America and a weekly critique group.

**Cheryl K. Pierson** ("Silver Magic") lives in Oklahoma City with her husband and two children. Cheryl, a freelance writer and novelist, is currently working on her third romance novel and is co-owner of FabKat Editorial Services, where she teaches workshops and weekly writing classes as well as edits manuscripts for other authors.

**Kathy L. Reed** ("Hollywood Holiday") is a writer and former high school mathematics teacher. She resides with her husband, Bruce, in Decatur, Alabama. Kathy has four grown children. In her spare time, she enjoys reading and playing the mountain dulcimer.

**Linda Rondeau** ("Santa's Reluctant Helper") resides in northern New York. Her work has appeared on the Internet as well as in various print publications and anthologies. Her book, *According to Daisy/Abundant Living for Moms,* will be released soon. Rondeau also contributes an inspirational, bi-weekly column for her hometown newspaper. Other writings may be viewed on her Web site, *www.lindarondeau.com.*

**Bob Rose** ("A Memorable Family Gathering") wears the hat of husband, father, and grandfather. He pastors a small church and operates an espresso shop, Higher Grounds, where he bakes homemade bagels, scones, and cookies.

**Marcia Rudoff** ("The Best Christmas Ever") is a freelance writer and memoir-writing teacher living in Bainbridge Island, Washington. Her work appears in various publications and several anthologies including *The Rocking Chair Reader: Family Gatherings* and *A Cup of Comfort for Inspiration*, as well as the *Bainbridge Island Review*, for which she writes a monthly column entitled *Senior Outlook*.

**Nan Schindler Russell** ("More than a Gift") is living her dream in Whitefish, Montana, after twenty years in management on the East Coast. Nan is a writer, columnist, small business owner, and instructor. Currently, she is writing her first book, *Winning at Working: 10 Lessons Shared*. More of Nan's work can be read at *www.nanrussell.com*.

**Candace Sams** ("Christmas with Peppermint") is a published, award-winning fiction author. She was a police officer for eleven years, an ambulance crew chief for eight, and she now lives in Alabama with her husband, Lee. She loves to hear from readers.

**Al Serradell** ("A Special Holiday Mass"), a Los Angeles native, is a veteran writing instructor in the Oklahoma City area. A professional journalist, he has worked for newspapers in Oklahoma (*The Journal Record, The Guthrie News Leader*) and Colorado (*The Rocky Mountain News*), and co-owns an editorial business, FabKat Editorial Services.

**Marilyn Mosher Shapley** ("Silver Bells") and her husband, Roland, operate their own business. Together they have four children and two grandchildren. Marilyn majored in English and creative writing, and minored in classical civilization. Her poems have been published in *New Delta Review* at Louisiana State University. She won first prize in poetry at Quincy College in Illinois, and she also has had a short story published in *Currents*,

St. Louis Community College at Meramec. Marilyn is a member of National Association of Women Writers.

**Micheale Collie Shelton** ("Wartime Sharing") has had a number of short stories accepted for publication. She has lived in Durham, North Carolina, for the past fifteen years with her husband, son, and daughter. Micheale has been engaged in creative writing since contracting rheumatoid arthritis and fibromyalgia, which left her disabled. Margaret Stanford Redmayne, her husband's grandmother, gave her permission for this story to be published.

**Wendy Stewart-Hamilton** ("It Isn't Much") is the founder of Inspired Life Ministries, Inc. and the Web site publisher for *www.InspiredMoms.com* and *www.InspiredParents.com*. She is married to Mike Hamilton, and together they parent three children, Kaile, Kayleigh, and Andrew, in Dallas, Texas.

**Mary Helen Straker** ("Faith"), formerly a newspaper and magazine reporter, has had her work published in both short fiction and nonfiction. She has had short stories published in the *A Cup of Comfort series* as well as *The Rocking Chair Reader series*. She is married to J. William Straker. They are the parents of three daughters and one son, and grandparents to eight grandchildren. Currently, Mary Helen is working on a family memoir that encompasses the years between 1793 and 1915.

**Donna Sundblad** ("Lighting of the Tree") is the author of the writing book, *Pumping Your Muse*. Donna also writes short stories, articles on the craft of writing including her monthly column *Birdie's Quill*, and conducts *Pumping Your Muse* workshops. She lives in southwestern Florida with her husband Rick and her flock of seven birds. Visit her Web site: *www.theinkslinger.net*.

**Wayne R. Wallace** ("A Bike for Christmas") is a fifty-eight-year-old university professor and fledgling writer, now retired following thirty-three years at the Oklahoma Gas & Electric Company. He has had several pieces of business and management curriculum published, but he continues to seek publication as a nontechnical writer.

**Suzanne Waring** ("Nothing Ever Happens in a Barn") retired in 2002 from her position as a college administrator and instructor, and then she turned her attention to freelance writing. Suzanne sold her first short story to the *Mature Years* magazine in December 2004, and she is presently completing a nonfiction book.

**Anne C. Watkins** ("Holiday on Ice") is the author of *The Conure Handbook* (Barron's Educational Series, Inc.), and her work has appeared in numerous print magazines and newspapers, selected Web sites, and in nearly forty anthologies. She and her husband, Allen, live in Vinemont, Alabama, where they love to spoil their grandchildren, Bailey, Chelsea, and Tyler. *www.geocities.com/anne_c_watkins*.

**Marian Webster** ("Silver-Dollar Christmas"). One door closes, another opens. After the death of her husband, Marian's opened door ushered her with passion and purpose into the world of writing. As a result, *Tina* was published in *Progenitor 2003*. Currently, Marian is on the final chapters of her first novel. She is seventy-three, lives in Castle Rock, Colorado, and still has river rafting on her to-do list. Marian's grandkids say, "Go for it, Grandma!"

**Karen Wilson** ("Mama's Gift") grew up on a dairy farm with four sisters and has lived in California her entire life. She has been happily married for thirty-two years and has two grown children. Karen loves writing inspirational articles.

**Wanda Winters-Gutierrez** ("A Basket of Straw") is an internationally published writer and poet, and she is the author of *The Search for Peace: A Women's Guide to Spiritual Wholeness*. Because of her multifaceted gifts, she is also known as an inspirational teacher of meditative journaling, an artist, and an entrepreneur, as well as a workshop and retreat leader.

**Ray Wong** ("A Brown and Yellow Christmas"), husband, and father of two, is a freelance writer who believes in the magic of words. His story is dedicated to all the teachers who make a difference in their students' lives each and every day.

**Leslie J. Wyatt** ("Now I Wonder . . . ") is a freelance writer with more than fifty articles and stories in publication. Her work appears in various anthologies including *A Cup of Comfort for Courage, My Heart's First Steps, The Rocking Chair Reader—Coming Home,* and *The Rocking Chair Reader—Memories from the Attic.* In addition, her middle-grade historical novel, *Poor Is Just a Starting Place,* is available from Holiday House Inc. Leslie conducts writing workshops and is a featured speaker for select events. She and her husband have been blessed with six children and live in a 1880s farmhouse in rural Missouri.